Now or Never

Personal Story Publishing Project Series

Bearing Up, 2018
- making do, bearing up, and overcoming adversity

Exploring, 2019
- discoveries, challenges, and adventures

That Southern Thing, 2020
- living, loving, laughing, loathing, leaving the South

Luck and Opportunity, sping 2021
- between if and if only

Trouble, fall 2021
- causing, avoiding, getting in, and getting out

Curious Stuff, spring 2022
- mementos, treasures, white elephants, and junk

Twists and Turns, fall 2022
- inflection points in life by choice, happenstance, misfortune, failure, and grace

Lost & Found, spring 2023
- loss and discovery—trials, serendipity, and life after

Sooner or Later, fall 2023
- about time, timing, and inevitability

Available through Daniel Boone Footsteps
www.danielboonefootsteps.com
www.RandellJones.com
1959 N. Peace Haven Rd., #105
Winston-Salem, NC 27106

Now or Never

Randell Jones, editor

Daniel Boone Footsteps
Winston-Salem, North Carolina

Copyrights retained by each writer for own stories
Permissions granted to Daniel Boone Footsteps
for publishing in this anthology

Compilation Copyright 2024, Daniel Boone Footsteps
All Rights Reserved

Daniel Boone Footsteps
1959 N. Peace Haven Rd., #105
Winston-Salem, NC 27106

RandellJones.com
DanielBooneFootsteps.com
DBooneFootsteps@gmail.com

Cover image courtesy of *Ansgar Koreng* / *CC BY-SA 4.0*

There are only so many tomorrows.
               — *Pope Paul VI*

Preface

This book is the tenth in a series of anthologies, collections of personal stories on a set theme, our Personal Story Publishing Project. Since beginning in 2018, our collections have included these titles:
Bearing Up,
Exploring,
That Southern Thing,
Luck and Opportunity,
Trouble,
Curious Stuff,
Twists and Turns,
Lost & Found, and
Sooner or Later.

This book comes from our 10th Call for Personal Stories, this one on the theme: "Now or Never—personal stories about courage and regrets, danger and desire, about choosing." We thank the scores of writers who responded to the call by submitting such interesting, thoughtful, and well-crafted stories. They delivered the diversity and depth of perspective we were hoping for and the insight to self which proved we chose the right theme. Each story is about 750-800 words, so the writers were challenged in executing their craft, telling an interesting story succinctly. The writers and we have all found the Personal Story Publishing Project through its ten iterations, so far, to be an instructive and rewarding writing experience. For the readers, it is a delight.

We received submissions from many writers in North Carolina and across the South, notably, but also from writers reaching across the country from Florida, Pennsylvania, and New York to the West Coast, with one expat now living in Chile. We wish we could have printed them all, but we are delighted to curate 41 stories for this collection.

In June 2019, we launched a second outlet for sharing these fine writers with a broader audience. Their work can now be heard in our twice weekly podcast, "6-minute Stories." Our podcast is available through Apple Podcasts (iTunes), Spotify, and Stitcher. You can listen directly to "6-minute Stories" and find all the stories archived at RandellJones.com/6minutestories. Episodes are announced on Facebook @6minutestories.

Now or Never, the Personal Story Publishing Project, and "6-minute Stories" podcast are undertaken by author and publisher Randell Jones, doing business as Daniel Boone Footsteps in Winston-Salem, North Carolina.

Thank you for enjoying and appreciating good storytelling. And, remember…
    Everybody loves a good story.^{sm} •

Contents

Preface vii
Contents .... ix-xiv
Introduction xv

Deadlines and Lifelines—My Healing Journey 1
    by Raven Chiong, Hayesville, NC
        – *The medical words rain down, soaking me to the core.*

Two Minutes and Eighteen Seconds 5
    by Richard L. Davis, Elk Grove, CA
        – *We did not want such a choice. Who would?*

Going on 3 9
    by Annette L. Brown, Atwater, CA
        – *Will I be a good grandmother?*

From Mudville to Joy Ville 13
    by Mary Alice Dixon, Charlotte, NC
        – *"You're not gonna get any last words from this one, Honey."*

Sitting Through Green 17
    by Jamie Cheshire, Winston-Salem, NC
        – *Truth is, she's sitting here beside me right now.*

Buffalo Plaid 21
    by Robin Russell Gaiser, Asheville, NC
        – *"You know one about grace or somethin'? My mama sang it."*

Shedding the Shoulds   25
    by Catherine Parisio, Calama, Chile
        — *His hand reached over and settled on my thigh.*

In Uncharted Territory   29
    by Alison Rice Bruster, Fort Mill, SC
        — *I felt as if I had entered nature's cathedral.*

Another Door   33
    by Lubrina Burton, Lexington, KY
        — *I took a deep breath.*

Parallel Universe   37
    by Lynne E Williams, Charlotte, NC
        — *20/20 hindsight and all that platitudinal crap*

Marsh Riches   41
    by Ginny Foard, Sullivan's Island, SC
        — *I am the sturdy jogger plodding along.*

What We Do   45
    by David Inserra, Hilton Head Island, SC
        — *"You guys are crazy."*

Getting a Head Start   49
    by Arlene Mandell, Linville, NC
        — *My excitement was contagious; I was hired on the spot.*

A Father's Dream   53
    by Thomas Gery, Reading, PA
        — *I was not dropping out; I was going in.*

Fit To Be Tied   57
    by Sandy Benson, Warne, NC
    — *"You're not gonna like this," he said.*

The Time Had Come   61
    by Ellen Zaroff, New York, NY
    — *It suddenly felt like I was chasing my tail.*

A Lost Curmudgeon   65
    by Akira Odani, St. Augustine, FL
    — *Should I call him? Is he asking for help?*

Perish the Thought   69
    by Kenneth Chamlee, Mills River, NC
    — *Quiet, please. This is a sacred space.*

Buck   73
    by M.J. Norwood, East Bend, NC
    — *"Hey! Mister! Throw me a ball! Hey! Mister!"*

Searching for Archibald   77
    by Phyllis Castelli, Henderson, NC
    — *"Where are all the old people?"*

Wild Things   81
    by Mick Scott, Winston-Salem, NC
    — *We see each other as we are.*

Horsehair in the Hummingbird Nest   85
    by Janet K. Baxter, Kings Mountain, NC
    — *Breeding for a silver dapple is a bit of a gamble.*

Modes and Memories   89
    by Edith Gettes, Asheville, NC
        — *He wore torment like a red velvet cape.*

Getting High on Second Chances   93
    by Ginny Grulke, Lexington, KY
        — *Technicolor visions rapidly appeared out of the haze.*

Green-eyed Lady, Not My Type   97
    by Bob Amason, St. Augustine, FL
        — *Her incantations were rhythmic and hypnotic.*

The News   101
    by Barbara Reese Yager, Fort Mill, SC
        — *"I have your back."*

Where Angels Fear   105
    by Cherie Cox, Charlotte, NC
        — *"I could have died happily in Florence."*

Then and Now   109
    by Patricia Joslin, Charlotte, NC
        — *It's time.*

Precious Treasure   113
    by Martha Rowe Vaughn, Mount Airy, NC
        — *Never was the real answer. I left disappointed and broken-hearted.*

A Drumbeat of Harp Strings   117
    by Annie Jenkins, Winston-Salem, NC
        — *the kind of naïve bravery I summoned to dare this experience*

Lifeguard — 121
    by Susan W. Harris, Hilton Head Island, SC
        — *I hesitated. I had never done a real rescue.*

One by One: Defying the "Nevers" — 125
    by Emily Rosen, Boca Raton, FL
        — *Oh, the lagging path between words and actions!*

The Storm Upstream — 129
    by Bill Donohue, Winston-Salem, NC
        — *to the palace and take the hill; Helen Keller on fire*

Out of Sight, Out of Mind? — 133
    by Erika Hoffman, Chapel Hill, NC
        — *Want to bet on that?*

Experiments in the Chemistry of Belonging — 137
    by Paula Teem Levi, Clover, SC
        — *Their excitement created more excitement.*

Do I Dare? — 141
    by Suzanne Cottrell, Oxford, NC
        — *I've got to get around it.*

Oh, My Son — 145
    by David Stern, Asheville, NC
        — *Everything is possible. Until it isn't.*

What If? — 149
    by Landis Wade, Charlotte, NC
        — *to risk failure as a writer*

You Done Gone This Far   153
    by Vicki Easterly, Frankfort, KY
    – *I even had dreams about it at night.*

Philadelphia Duval: Taking the Plunge   157
    by C. J. Munson, Winston-Salem, NC
    – *She chose freedom.*

The Passing   161
    by Randell Jones, Winston-Salem, NC
    – *"Goodbye, Horace."*

Introduction

It's now or never, we sometimes think. And so, we leap... *Time waits for no one. No guts, no glory!* Our philosophies and folk lore are full of admonitions and encouragements to act and to act now. So, we are off in a flash—perhaps.

But as quickly as we consider all the reasons *why*, we are niggled by the *why nots—Better safe than sorry. Fools rush in.* That sort of thing. So, we hold back. We think and reconsider. We are in a quandary wondering which way to go, whom to choose, what to do now. And we are haunted as well by the specter of later looking back with regret and wondering, *What if only I had ... (fill in the blank)?*

But take heart. In that quandary lies evidence of our values, our predilections, our druthers, and also our recollections of what our elders told us we *ought* to do. How close we heed them, however, is another matter. Knowing what to do and doing it are indeed different matters. Thus, our quandaries are the seed beds for the stories we tell about our *now-or-nevers*.

But *now* and *never* are not always a choice. Each word stands on its own as a state of being. With *now*, we are in the present, dealing with what *is*, reality staring us hard eye-to-eye. And in *never*, we perhaps face finality, the end of something. Be it dreaded, bothersome, or deeply loved, it is no more.

Mostly though, when we ponder *now or never*, we reminisce and consider our lives as a series of choices. And looking back we see the points at which we made important diversions from one path onto another which is why we are where we are and why we are who we are. And we have our stories to tell.

We are delighted by the response to our tenth Call for Personal Stories, and we are thankful to all the writers who invested time and energy into crafting personal stories for possible inclusion in this anthology. From among the submissions, we chose stories to include based on the quality of the writing and the resonance of the personal experiences shared with the announced theme, "Now or Never—personal stories about courage and regret, danger and desire, about choosing."

We have stories about endings, our struggles with disease and the coming to terms with what will be a different life, a shorter life than we might have hoped for. We have, as well, stories about such endings brought on willfully and the impacts and effects those passings have for the loved ones remaining, be they spouses, parents, friends, colleagues. We have stories of connections made at deathbedsides that touched those attending with new revelations for them.

We have stories of challenges made and challenges taken, some in the emotional soup of adolescence, some hearing the voice of an elder's expectations, some from the desperation of being trapped in a going-nowhere routine, and others from the wisdom of years when committed actions count for more than myriad insincere declarations.

We have stories of the unexpected—a literal windfall of dollars, a pilfered Bible delivered to a mailbox as an act of "ought-to-be" justice, a baseball tossed to a fan who remembered a favored nickname, and a lingering thoughtful encounter with a stranger who becomes more recognizable the longer one ponders the similarities.

We have stories of self-discovery—affirmation of readiness for a new life role from an unlikely young seatmate, building deep, new friendships among fellow adventurers half-way around the globe, understanding that magic and novelty are just not wild enough, accepting that music played from the heart soothes grief better than perfection ever could, and realizing that doing what is "good for me" is honest self-care.

Some stories are about searching for our ancestors and our elders, bring those we will never meet into our *now*, perhaps imbuing them with qualities we would like for ourselves, or affirming that the love we witnessed between them across a lifetime was deeply rooted for a reason, or at least confirming their whereabouts so we can remember them in a place and time and visit them there when we might.

Introduction

We have writers recalling how they got started in their craft in high school with the right type of skill, and how a second-act interest blossomed into more than a pastime and became a passion, and how sometimes being where a reporter needs to be to get the story they want can leave them out in the cold.

Other stories are shared by those who are glad they took their chances—to breed a new colt a dozen years in advance of enjoying it, to start a new business no one else had ever done, to reach back openly when family reaches out from a long silence, to hike back down into the dry, hot canyon to help a stranger, to save the life of a 10-year boy, and to experiment with marijuana 50 years later than your peers.

This collection includes stories of teachers who stayed on for a while after they had decided to leave and discovered their true calling and passion. We have a story of world treasures in trouble from tourists and one of a daughter troubled by the lack of a parallel world created just in time for her mother.

These are some of the stories among all those we share in this collection. We think our writers have brought their best for you to read and to consider. On matters of courage and desire, danger and regret, the following stories are offered to you.

It's time to get started, yes? Now or never. •

RJ

Deadlines and Lifelines
—My Healing Voyage
by Raven Chiong

Respectfully submitted November 23, 2023
with floodtides of gratitude this Thanksgiving Day

I've always been a lover of words but hearing "non-small cell adenosarcoma of the lung" in January 2023 the week of my fifty-ninth birthday were words I could literally live without. *Stage Four.* Two more words that rocked my world. *Who me?* I thought lifelong endurance athletes, running coaches, vegetarians, and non-smokers were immune. The medical words rain down, soaking me to the core, drenching me in a deep sea of disbelief. This past year has been a year of mostly calm desperation, casting my own lifeline to save myself in a tempest tossed with waves washing over me. Here I am, nearly a year later, still standing on dry land, shaking myself off, undrowned.

Survival is nothing new. I learned how to take care of myself at age 5 in my broken, multiracial family of origin. My biological father, a sailor above all else, abandoned his family leaving us to fend for ourselves. I began my writing career that same year when I became a pen pal to my cash-strapped, overburdened, absent mother who worked full time to feed and clothe her four children. Pen and paper connected us like an umbilical cord, unsevered. Running and writing have been my survival tools. I've lived a fearless life, relying on my still, small voice for guidance and protection and guardian angels who've thrown lifelines when I needed them the most.

I've overcome eating disorders and clinical depression.

I've survived near electrocution, falling redwood trees, and triggering an avalanche in the Trinity Alps. I've fractured my fingers, toes, ribs, and pelvis. In 1988, I was hit by a car while riding my mountain bike. When my un-helmeted head struck the pavement, the impact sounded like a gunshot. As I awaited help, Gladys Knight and the Pips affirmed "I Will Survive" through my Sony Walkman headphones. I've long realized that someone else besides my biological father has had my back and now my lungs, too.

This latest dis-*ease* is a medical diagnosis, not my truth. My heart is open to the wisdom of the Ancient Ones who knew that food is medicine. I've consciously chosen the route less travelled: zero sugar, high alkaline, low glycemic, whole foods and Tai Chi, Qi Gong, Jin Shin Jyutsu, energy treatments, vitamin supplements, acupuncture, traditional Chinese medicine, breathwork, rebounding, massage, and digital detoxing. Tibetan and Native American flute sound therapy round out my healing regimen. My seven rescue dogs are good medicine, too. I do not walk alone.

Still, I write between bouts of pain, riding the latest healing crisis of chronic coughing, debilitating exhaustion, and weight loss. My jeans slide off my hips as my weight plummets to all time adult lows. New lumps and bumps are found. The word "deadline" takes on a new meaning. How much time remains to live, to write?

The tides are turning, I can tell. I no longer stand in the Blue Ridge Mountains longing for the ocean. The place I thought I left behind resides within. Saltwater flows through my veins. It's in my DNA. I can taste it in my tears. I am the sea, and the sea is me. No separation.

This is no time for throwing in the ropes. May it not be said that I fought and battled the "C-word." Rather, one with the ocean of benevolence, I rode her ebbs and flows, followed the path of stars and moonlight on water, followed the lighthouse perched within. I know the way, and I must stay on course. I remain the captain of my ship, sacred vessel, ephemeral container of my soul. Cure is not the same as healing. Death is not a failure. Courage and a boat load of gratitude are required to ply these choppy, uncharted waters. No one promised an easy journey. Robert Moss casts the latest lifeline. His online class, "Embracing Death, Dying, and the Afterlife Using Shamanic Practices and Dream Work" assures me of the Life After Life I know to be true. Medicine Pipe, my powerful energy healer, holds my hand and heart as I stand, unwavering, at the helm.

In traditional Chinese medicine, the lungs are the container for grief and sadness. Thus, the missing piece. Peace. It's time now to ride the winds and waves to the Island of Forgiveness. It's time now to harness and transmute the wounds my father left in his wake. They are, indeed, the gifts that promise safe passage to the great beyond. There is no other way around the rocky shore. It's time now to be set free.

Anchors aweigh! •

Copyright 2024, Raven Chiong

Raven Chiong earned her Master of Arts in Exercise and Sport Science from the University of Florida. A lifelong student, life coach, and educator, she qualified for the first-ever Women's Olympic Marathon Trials in 1984 and paid it forward with her nineteen-year cross country coaching career. After her competitive running and coaching career, she ran her pen across the pages of this life. Raven is the author of *Ode to the Still, Small Voice—A Memoir of Listening*. She is the proud mother to four rescue dogs.

Editor's note:
Raven Chiong passed away at home December 11, 2023, at 8:00 p.m., surrounded by her family.

Two Minutes and Eighteen Seconds
by Richard L. Davis

Circles are meant to be complete. But sometimes a gap remains, and the reciprocal curves of the arc never quite close. Something always remains missing, unfinished. Love can be like that, as can life itself. For my wife and me, our dreams together promised a complete circle, a generous, happy life of love fulfilled. But sometimes …

We had planned for our 50th wedding anniversary some dozen years hence, to round out and celebrate the marvelous life we shared. But it was not to be. She fell ill with breast cancer. It had teased her for decades, and then it was here. Treatment followed—surgery, chemo, radiation. Then it returned a second time. More treatments. Then again. Each time, worse, and worse.

The disease spread to her bone marrow, then to ulcers on her skin. Her capillaries thinned, leading to spontaneous and copious bleeding. Surgery took the lymph nodes in her armpits, and lymphedema swelled her arms until her left hand became useless. A recurring uncertainty appeared in her eyes. With her body now so damaged and distorted, she no longer felt … lovable. Even more, her eyes showed a fear that she would face the disease alone. But I was going nowhere. If anything, she needed me now more than ever.

In what would become her final summer, her oncologist shared the "good" news that the disease was killing her slowly. Then he added the bad news—that it was killing her slowly. He suggested she consider a "physician-assisted solution," legal in California.

We did not want such a choice. Who would? We loved each other in ways we both knew yet could never quite explain to others, even though others somehow seemed to see it.

We hoped to keep the news just between the two of us at first, but more doctors would be involved. Her oncologist asked that she meet alone with a consulting physician to show that no one manipulated her choice. I took her to the appointment and waited outside, patient, committed, curious.

Her mother had died of colon cancer, with surgeries that opened her abdomen. She lived for months like that. As a teenager at the time, all my wife now remembered was the pain and cries of the mother she loved. And the odor.

She did not want to end like that.

We learned of new drugs—the first, a pill, a sedative to relax the throat and prevent regurgitation of the second, a lethal drug. A pharmacist taught me how to mix the latter. The "potion" I called it. The "kill pill," she called it. She also had to take both drugs by herself and—importantly—be able to swallow four ounces of the final potion within less than two minutes—all of it in 120 seconds. The whole thing felt surreal, academic, clinical.

Then the day came when she could barely swallow anything—food or drink.

She began to pull away from me, to distance herself. I kissed her, and she did not kiss back. I held her hand, squeezed it, but she did not squeeze in return. Even our smiles had slipped into memory. Too soon. My eyes pleaded with her, my heart in my throat. "I don't do goodbyes," she said. No goodbyes for me, for us—for *Our Us*. No goodbyes for our decades, our lifetime, of love and hellos. She had made her choice and kept asking for the kill pill.

The moment came. Still abed, she took the sedative pill with some difficulty, gagging somewhat as she swallowed. As we waited for the requisite one-hour interval to pass between dosages, I prepared the final potion. With great effort, she sat up to the edge of her bed. Still not holding my hand or looking at me, she nodded; and I yielded the kill pill to her. Her whole being focused on what she needed to do.

I started my stopwatch as she took her first sip. She drank with steady persistence and swallowed without difficulty, pausing only once to take a short breath. The emptied glass slipped into my hand, and I stopped the watch. I laid her back on the bed and closed her eyelids. A small blanket covered her from neck to ankles, leaving her pretty feet exposed. I caressed them, already cold, lifeless. She looked asleep, her head rolled to one side, her mouth open.

Thus we marked an end to our still unfinished circles of life and love together. I caressed her feet again, feeling each toe, remembering how I had loved every part of her. Heart and soul.

I looked at my stopwatch. Our circles of love and life together were put to rest after two minutes and eighteen seconds. •

Copyright 2024, Richard L. Davis

Richard ("Rick") Davis is a retired Air Force colonel with an extensive professional writing history, including some non-fiction material published over the past 40 years. To transition to fiction, he studied with Amherst Writers & Artists and published his first novella in 2014. He has two book-length manuscripts pending. "Two Minutes and Eighteen Seconds" marks his second offering to PSPP, which earlier accepted his submission for *Lost & Found* (spring 2023). He lives in Elk Grove, California, with his Himalayan cat, Phoebe, and memories of his wife, Myra.

Going on 3
by Annette L. Brown

I said yes without hesitation. Now I'm hesitant.

Feet shuffle in the aisle. Carry-ons scrape into overheads —background music to the questions on loop in my mind: *Do I remember how to care for an infant? Will I be a good grandmother?* Apprehension has tucked itself in my pocket as I travel to care for my three-month-old grandchild. It's only for one week—help as my daughter-in-law returns to work. But I haven't changed a diaper in … *oh, my.*

The dropped backpack and his shimmy into his seat interrupt my disquiet. My new seatmate raises slender arms and swings them back and forth, loosely like willow branches caught in conflicting breezes. He snaps his fingers at the edge of each swing. I lean toward the window. Six-year-old arms aren't very long, but everything in an airplane is tight.

I smile. "What's your name?"

Sable eyes stretch round, "Zowhat in English, Joel (ho-wel) in Spanish!" He punctuates each word with a head bob.

"Hello, Zowhat. I'm Annette." We shake hands.

"I hope you're okay sitting by him." Zowhat's aunt introduces herself from across the aisle; his older sister sits next to her. "He's active."

The flight is only 90 minutes. "We'll be fine."

He wrestles his seatbelt. When I offer help, he nods and shares white teeth framed in walnut cheeks.

During takeoff, he clutches the armrest. "I'm so nervous." Each word achieves a higher pitch.

"We'll be fine." I pat his hand.

Later, head bent, neck craned, he scours his backpack for entertainment. I open the Powerade drink he finds.

He slowly but accurately sounds out words from his books in English (versus his books in Spanish). I praise him.

He declares, "I know to my 7s!" Bounce …bounce … bounce—his bottom hitting the seat creates his counting rhythm: "1. 2. 3. 4. 5. 7!"

"Wait! Zowhat! 6 is heartbroken! Forgotten! Skipped! How could you do that to 6?" I thrust hand to heart.

Zowhat's brows furrow. Then his eyes shoot open, and he throws both hands over his mouth, flutter-kicking his legs. "Let me redo!"

We high-five his correction.

When we play Rochambeau, he tries to cheat by changing his

rock to paper or scissors just after I reveal my choice.

"No!" He encloses my ready hands with his. "We go on 'go,' not on '3'! 1, 2, 3, go! Then you go. You have to do it right." He holds my gaze, lips pressed together—not cheating, playing at a different rhythm.

I watch Zowhat drink his Powerade like it's a sporting event: tilt-to-the-right, almost spill, tilt-to-the-left, almost spill. I don't say anything. When he finally tilts too far, I grab his hand and hold the bottle upright as he exclaims, "Oh no! Oh no! Sorry!" I tell him I've been saving my napkins just in case. He looks worried.

"You won't melt!" I wink as I dab the backpack. He laughs.

He tells me he's in kindergarten. "I have two teachers. My English teacher is Ms. Marin." Then in a voice stretched with feeling he adds, "Oh, I love her—so much," emphasizing his declaration with waving arms and snaps. When I ask about his Spanish teacher, he reports, "Mr. Lopez."

I wait. He stares straight ahead, sits still.

Okay, then.

We look out the window, declare the clouds look like cotton, popcorn, rabbit fur, pillow fluff, bouncy balls.

During the descent, the plane lurches from turbulence. I grab the armrest. He says, "We'll be fine." Then he pats my hand.

I help him gather his belongings. He stands, faces down the aisle, but turns back. I slide toward the aisle but remain seated,

Going on 3

so we are eye to eye. He lunges toward me.

"Thank you, Zowhat, for being such a fun flightmate!" The feel of his small arms wrapped around my neck warms me.

I watch his backpack bounce away and think about my lie—well, half-truth. Of course, Zowhat was fun. But as he arranged himself on the seat before takeoff, I did not realize he would be one of those people who comes into your life for a week, a day, a few hours—sometimes you don't even remember their names—but they address a need. Archetypal heroes typically meet a helper-guide who gives them gifts, often knowledge. I guess I'm the hero of my story, who received wisdom from an unlikely source, a 6-year-old who shared his fear, love, and joy openly in response to my interest and who reminded me children show us who they are and what they need if we are paying attention.

I leave the plane assured that my grandson will be open to my touch and comforted by my kind words, that he will appreciate my attempts at play and know I'm trying, that he will forgive my mistakes—like when I go on "3" instead of on "go." •

Copyright 2024, Annette L. Brown

Annette L. Brown is a mother, wife, and retired teacher, who lives on an almond farm in Central California where she enjoys spending time with family and friends. She is grateful for the support of The Taste Life Twice Writers and The Light Makers' Society and for simply having time to write. Annette has pieces reflecting her love of nature, family, beauty, and humor in several publications including *Cathexis Northwest Press*, *Last Stanza Poetry*, *Flash Fiction Magazine*, *Every Day Fiction*, and other PSP Project anthologies.

From Mudville to Joy Ville
by Mary Alice Dixon

"Mr. Doc's a goner," the nurse tells me. "Never open his eyes again. You're not gonna get any last words from this one, Honey." She shrugs, walks out of the Memory Care Activity Center, a pale pink room where the activity consists mostly of staff emptying catheter bags between rounds of *Joy to the World* sing-alongs to which few patients sing along. *Joy to the World* in July? In North Carolina? No wonder the patients are confused.

I look at Doc. He had never been a doctor. Not unless you count how he used to doctor his garden soil with potato peels and cow manure. Now he lies motionless on a metal frame hospital bed. His 97-year-old body is a landscape of bones. Eyes shut, chest rattling, lips blue.

Doc once told me folks thought he lived alone but he said he didn't. Not really. He said he lived with the dirt under his nails, the seed catalogs on his shelves and the Bible on his table.

Years ago, he had a booth at the Charlotte Regional Farmers Market. He claimed his were the sweetest tomatoes, the crispest carrots, the ripest squash. Said the secret was in the mud.

"Doc, you grew the juiciest tomatoes." I take his hand.

From Mudville to Joy Ville

"Remember those Big Boys?"
No response.

An aide starts another chorus of *Joy to the World*.

"Remember Christmas at the Farmers Market?"
No response.

I rub a wet sponge on Doc's lips then look at the green Jello untouched on his dinner tray.

"Doc? Want some Jello?"
No response.

"Okay, let's read." I pull books out of my bag. "*Glory be to God for Dappled Things*. Gerard Manley Hopkins."

The nurse returns, frowning. "Honey, that man has no schooling."

I take a deep breath. The air reeks of coconut air freshener and stale urine. I read Hopkins.
No response.

"How about Robert Louis Stevenson? Swings, cows, and counterpanes?" Doc wheezes.

A woman in a wheelchair shakes her head. "Mr. Doc can't hear you. Just pray over him."

I thumb through my volume of *Best Loved Poems*.
"Here's *The Lord is my Shepherd*." My voice shakes as
I chant the Twenty-Third Psalm.
Doc's eyes stay closed. I turn the page.
"Let's try *Casey at the Bat*."

Written in 1888 by Ernest Thayer, *Casey* is a long ballad of 52 lines in 13 stanzas. It's the story of the hometown baseball team, the Mudville Nine, in the final inning of a game. Mudville is losing. The "mighty Casey," Mudville's champion slugger, is their last hope.

I get to the fifth stanza when Casey is sent in to bat, "then from 5,000 throats and more there rose a lusty yell…."

At the words "lusty yell" Doc opens his eyes.

"Oh my God, you're awake?"

"Ten thousand eyes were on him," Doc says, quoting the first line of the poem's seventh stanza, "as he rubbed his hands with dirt."

I drop my book. I lean into Doc's face, cup his chin in my hands. "Doc?"

He doesn't answer. Not directly. But in a steady voice Doc recites every single word of every single line for the next 27 lines of *Casey at the Bat*. Perfectly, word for word.

He gets to the end: "Oh somewhere in this favored land the sun is shining bright… somewhere hearts are light… somewhere men are laughing, and somewhere children shout…."

Then Doc delivers the poem's final line: "But there is no joy in Mudville—mighty Casey has struck out." Mudville loses. Doc laughs.

I feel the brush of angel wings. I've heard of people rallying in their last moments, terminal lucidity, it's called. But I've never witnessed it. Until now.

From Mudville to Joy Ville

"Doc?"

He locks eyes with me. "My father."

"Your father?"

"My father, a schoolteacher. Taught me Mudville is here. Joy Ville is there. Goodbye, Mudville. I'm home running to Joy Ville. Lots of innings up there."

Doc falls silent. He dies peacefully.

The next morning, watering my backyard tomatoes, I feel a sudden certainty that I would never have gotten a glimpse of Doc's Joy Ville if I hadn't stumbled into reading *Casey at the Bat* at just the right moment. Then I spot something on the ground. It's a baseball covered with mud. It looks like it's been there a while. But I never noticed it before.

Or maybe, just maybe, Doc hit it out of the park last night. Miracles do happen. Christmas is six months away, but I hum a few bars from *Joy to the World*, grateful for having known the man with dirt under his nails and extra innings in his heaven. In my Mudville, this day, there is joy. •

Copyright 2024, Mary Alice Dixon

Mary Alice Dixon is a Pushcart nominee, award-winning poet and former finalist for the NC Poetry Society Poet Laureate Award. Her writing is in five PSPP anthologies, in *Braided Way*, *County Lines*, *Kakalak*, *Main Street Rag*, *Pinesong*, and elsewhere. Her poetry will appear on NC Poetry Society posters in 2024. Mary Alice lives in Charlotte, NC, where she teaches a Hospice Grief Writing Workshop for the bereaved. Her course includes found poems, tears, laughter, peppermint candy and plenty of blueberry scones. She also collects old stories and loves old hats.

Sitting Through Green
by Jamie Cheshire

The first thing I noticed was what looked like clown shoes. But that couldn't be right. Not here. Not today anyway. I was about a half block away and, as I got closer, I realized I was looking at the mismatched attire of poverty and fatigue.

It was Sunday morning, and I was pulling up to the light at MLK and Cleveland. A woman on the sidewalk had crossed Cleveland from the McDonald's on that corner and looked like she was going to come on across MLK. But she was moving delicately and ponderously slow. Arthritically slow.

I had stopped on red and could see her easily.

The shoes were fluffy scuffs and their tall profile ahead of her skinny ankles gave her feet the comical poise I'd seen at a distance. I was already fascinated with her—another ordinary citizen of the active and fringy intersections around this contrasted little proud town.

Other than her feet—which told their own story—I was fascinated with the deep lavender head cloth she wore, folded and wrapped into a self-possessed nobility and worn as well as any royalty could, and her bright, gold, billowy sweatshirt. But what further caught my eye and held it was the color of her skin. I should say its light. It was the color of my coffee when it's right but it had a honeyed glow no coffee has ever had. A glow undiminished by recognizably mean circumstance.

The ordinary person crossing in front of me was beautiful.

She started across MLK near the white lines that told her where to walk but dismissed their instructions and took the shorter path. Just a little jaywalk because those white lines offered her nothing. And she paid no attention to the man in the white truck, stopped at this particular moment, at this particular light while driving over to the next town to have breakfast with his son. She was squinting at a voice I could hear back behind me to my left and seemed not to even see me, dividing her attention between the voice, her careful steps, the lines, and my truck. I was just another object she had to navigate.

I was just another object. An obstacle. A thing between her and where she was going.

The veil fluttered open a little and I could clearly see the scraped and fragile uncertainty of her circumstance. For an instant, the way she carried her coffee became its most visible symbol. She cradled it from the bottom, the way one does when take-out coffee is too hot. But she carried it carefully, attentively, as if it were precious.

NOW OR NEVER

Was she going to sit and have coffee with the voice behind
me? Did they have a regular place? A sunny place? Would they
smoke? Was one coffee intended for two? What might they
talk about? Or who?

The veil fell all the way away from both appearances, the
beautiful and the poor, leaving neither. What do I know about
this woman? What entire, happy or unhappy, vivid life is
looking out from the eyes squinted at the voice behind me
to my left, squinted so deep they're just black crinkles under
her brow? What work and what play have engaged the hands
now holding that hot cup? Have they known tenderness?
What is her story? Who are her people? Are they near?
How long have her feet felt the way they feel today?
How did she get here?

And how did I?

When I looked up, the light was just turning yellow to tell me
I had sat through green and that time had stopped again
to show me something I could not otherwise have seen.
I wondered how many changes I'd sat through. How big
a minute had been held out?

She rode with me then, all the way to Greensboro, just as
certainly as if she had been beside me in the truck. And when
Ryan and I were done with breakfast and the errands he
needed, she caught a ride back. Truth is, she's sitting here
beside me right now.

Sitting Through Green

On the ride back she said, *You know that thing some people say when they see somebody looks like me?* She waited. *I know you know it. 'There, but for the grace of God, go I?'*

I've been thinking a lot lately about the stories we tell ourselves about ourselves and about the differences between us.
I nodded and looked over at her. She was watching me hear what she was saying.

That's not the truth, she said.

I waited.

There go I. That's the truth. •

Copyright 2024, Jamie Cheshire

Fascinated with every big and little thing, Jamie Cheshire has long been an avid student of design and structure. Having worked together with giants, he has had the extreme good fortune to practice his craft for most of the last four decades and has seen his graphic work appear nationally and in several countries on three continents. He lives in Winston-Salem, North Carolina, with his beloved feral, hippie-chick wife, their three dogs and two cats. Deeply committed to the ordinary, he is constantly searching for a way to describe it.

Editor's note: MLK is Martin Luther King, Jr. Drive in Winston-Salem, N.C.

Buffalo Plaid
by Robin Russell Gaiser

Doug sat alone in his room. His beige recliner was angled sideways so he could stare out the expansive window to the deep snowy woods. His door was partially open. No television or radio played. He wasn't reading or working a puzzle or talking on the phone like other patients. The head nurse suggested I go to his room. He never had visitors. I was the Certified Music Practitioner at Mountain Valley Hospice in upstate New York.

"He might refuse you, but it's worth a try," she said.

When I knocked lightly on his door, he jerked around and scowled through bushy gray eyebrows. I braced myself for a blast of cuss words demanding me to get out. Instead, he said nothing and continued to scowl at me. A quilted flannel buffalo plaid shirt, the usual red and black checks, thread-bare blue jeans, and untied tan work boots with the leather laces dangling to the floor shouted the language of an outdoor, working man. I looked more closely and noticed missing fingers on his hand as it lay across his lap. *Lumberjack*, I thought.

The vast unforgiving Adirondack Mountains harbor many a

hard-living man eking out a meager living in the woods just five hours north of New York City.

I approached the solitary mountain man slowly. Keeping my distance, I slid my harmonica from my pants pocket, and showed it to him.

"Hi Doug, I'm Robin, the Hospice musician. Would you like a little music today? I'm not offended if you say no. And you can tell me to stop anytime." He studied me and my harmonica then nodded his head ever so slightly. I began playing "Get Along Home, Cindy, Cindy," an upbeat folk tune often played on hammer dulcimer in the lumber camps. His scowl softened, but he resumed staring out the window. I finished the tune, stood there in silence, about to ask him if he wanted more music.

I didn't expect him to speak first.

"My uncle played one a' them," he said flatly, looking at me briefly, then turning his head toward the window again.

"You want me to play some more?"

"Yeah," he said still looking away.

I played more camp tunes, "Golden Slippers," "I Been Workin' on the Railroad," "Oh, Susannah." When I stopped and pushed the harmonica into my pocket, he spoke again.

"When you comin' back?"

"Next week."

"Good."

The following week I tapped on his door before entering. He sat in his chair by the window, clad in the same outfit, but his expression changed to a crooked smile when he looked around and saw me. I pulled up a chair, but not too close to him, lifted my guitar out of its case and sang country music: Johnny Cash, Elvis, Loretta. He listened facing the window with the view of the woods. After several songs he spoke in the same flat tone.

"You know one about grace or somethin'? My mama sang it."

I began playing the intro to "Amazing Grace." While I sang the first verse, I briefly glanced at him, making sure he was okay. I noticed tears in his eyes. He swallowed hard.

Music reaches deeply into memory and sometimes evokes overwhelming emotion. When that occurs with patients, I know from my therapeutic music classes and my experience to change the song or stop the music altogether. Doug's reaction didn't alarm me, so I sang all four remaining verses, still monitoring his responses.

Doug welcomed my music for weeks, but I began to notice telltale signs that he was failing. He slept more; some days he was not fully dressed. His favorite snacks, Pepsi and cheese crackers, were left uneaten on the side table by his chair.

It was a typical Adirondack winter day: penetratingly cold with

Buffalo Plaid

heavy gray skies spitting snow. On days like that I yearned to stay put, cozy in our home by the lake. But something pushed me to dress, don my Hospice badge and drive the sixteen miles to Hospice.

When I entered Doug's room, he was lying in a raised hospital bed, breathing irregularly, and non-responsive. His hand with the missing fingers lay across his chest. No buffalo plaid shirt or worn jeans or work boots anywhere. The nurses had covered him with a dark green fleece blanket adorned with pine trees, deer, bears.

Leaning in closer to him, I softly improvised music on my harmonica. My breath caught more than once as I played and studied this private woodsman who had allowed me into his life.

Little did I know, at the time, that the music I gave him that day was the last sound he heard on this earth. •

Copyright 2024, Robin Gaiser

Robin Russell Gaiser, MA, CMP, added a certificate for music practitioner to her degrees in English literature and psychology. As an experienced multi-instrumentalist and vocalist, Robin gave live bedside acoustic music to critically and chronically ill, elderly and dying patients in hospices, hospitals, rehabs, nursing and private homes. Her first book, *Musical Morphine: Transforming Pain One Note at a Time* (Pisgah Press, 2016) chronicles such work. Her second book, *Open for Lunch* (Pisgah Press, 2018) offers readers a look at what happened when Robin asked random diners to join her for lunch. She and her husband live in Asheville, North Carolina. www.robingaiser.com

Shedding the Shoulds
by Catherine Parisio

When his hand reached over and settled on my thigh, I knew what I *should* do. I *should* forcefully remove his hand and confidently stomp out the door. When his gaze caught mine and an impish grin crept across his face, I knew what I *should* feel. I *should* feel offended, indignant, violated. But I felt none of those things.

Instead, the pace of my heart doubled. I felt the heat rising in my body, the all-encompassing awareness of him. The sweat glands in my armpits swelled to bursting, and I'm sure my freckled face flushed crimson. Outwardly I kept my cool, as I imagined a 20-year-old adult would. I held his gaze for a beat, gave him my own knowing smile, and flirtatiously placed his hand back in his lap. "Dr. R., we have work to do."

I returned to the computer screen, though precisely categorizing pigeon behavior no longer held my attention. I felt his touch again. "Has anyone ever told you you have great legs?" Pleased with my choice of skintight leggings, I flashed another smile his way, while my brain furiously raced through my options. Do I follow the dictates of my conservative Catholic upbringing and shut this down? Or do I heed the message coursing through my body, screaming for me to take the risk?

Dr. R. had been on my radar ever since I developed a giant-sized, coed crush on him in my sophomore year. The unconventional, motorcycle-riding, leather jacket-wearing professor with a PhD from Harvard conducted his classes with a charisma and energy not commonly found on university grounds. Although we had never spoken a word, I was hooked.

When that term ended, I tried to banish him from my mind. That kind of romance was the stuff of movies, not real life.

The following year, I needed an advisor. I was reluctant to ask Dr. R., worried my crush would only be distracting. However, as the head of the department of my chosen specialty, he was the natural choice.

That's how I found myself working alone in a windowless, closet-sized office with Dr. R. at my side, a year's worth of unrealized desire silencing the little voice telling me what I *should* do. I let his hand stay.

He suggested dinner. We sped towards the coast on his motorcycle, my body wrapped behind his, arms enveloping his waist. The feel of the air on my face coupled with the reality of him in my arms filled me with giddy bliss.

I was relieved the restaurant was deserted; the specter of *should* lingering on the edge of my mind. Although the university was a big one and we were both adults, the taboos surrounding professors and students wasn't lost on me.

Despite the differences between us, our conversation flowed

easily. While we waited for the check, Dr. R. swung himself around the table and scooched close, draping an arm around me. I pushed away any thoughts about what I *should* feel and do. I *wanted* this. I felt viscerally, intensely alive. As we zipped back to campus, I pressed my body close to his, taboos be damned. Why should society dictate what I should and shouldn't do?

After returning the helmets to his office, I started immediately for the door, nervous about the impending goodbye. But Dr. R. caught my hand and pulled me close. His intense gaze both thrilled and unnerved me. He leaned in and delivered a gentle yet intoxicating kiss that left me wanting more. I put up a restraining hand. I was still figuring out my boundaries, and I wanted to make sure Dr. R. would respect those, which he did.

The next day, I couldn't focus on my schoolwork as the details of the night replayed in my mind. I didn't know where this was going, but I wanted to find out.

With the term ending, I needed some feedback on my final paper. Dr. R. and I arranged a time to meet: his house, 9 o'clock Tuesday night. I didn't consciously consider the implications, but as I shaved my legs, curled my hair and selected a flattering outfit for our "meeting," I couldn't claim to be unaware of the possibilities.

Standing at his front door that night, my whole body lit up. Before I knocked, the *shoulds* crept back. I *should* go home. I *should* reschedule during office hours. But what was wrong with listening to my heart, my desires? I made a decision that night, a resolution that became a pivotal conviction throughout my life: What I *should* do is follow my own path, do what is right for me.

I knocked and stepped inside. I knew I might be setting myself up for embarrassment, heartbreak, or disappointment, but I was okay with that. I was seizing the moment, and no matter what happened, this story would be mine. •

Copyright 2024, Catherine Pariso

Catherine Parisio is a freelance editor, relentless writer, and international schoolteacher, currently living and working in Calama, Chile. The college student with the courage to take a risk and pursue an unconventional relationship became a woman living a somewhat uncommon life as an international schoolteacher, seizing opportunities to experience all that life has to offer. Catherine believes the pivotal moments of life provide insight into the core values that shape us; writing and sharing these stories is an intimate act that reveals our humanity.

In Uncharted Territory
by Alison Rice Bruster

The air was still and slightly cool. Water lapped on the rocks at the sides of the cave. As my eyes adjusted to the darkness, I leaned back in the life ring that held me afloat and took in the contours of the space around me.

The water was azure blue and as clear as a pane of glass. It appeared to be lit from below, almost like a swimming pool with underwater lights. It took me a minute to grasp what was creating the vivid color. Concentrated light was entering through the narrow opening, being refracted through the water like a prism, and bouncing off the bottom of the cave.

It was early, so we were practically the only people in the grotto just then. Our whole group of nine had made an initial foray in the dinghy. Then three of us swam the distance back from where our boat was anchored to the opening of the cave, wearing life rings for support.

Once inside, all conversation stopped; we were each lost in our thoughts. The only noises were the soft splash of the waves pushing in under the rocks near the opening and the sound of our breathing.

I felt like I had entered nature's cathedral. The roof of the cave soared above us, several stories up, like an irregular set of gothic arches made of craggy stone. The cave wall included a large indentation across from the opening that resembled a high altar. Niches in the side walls made me think of the chapels dedicated to saints in a Catholic church.

And this dim, enclosed space did feel like a sanctuary somehow; like we were hidden away and shielded from anything that may have been pressing down on us in our lives outside.

As I floated and looked around me, I thought of how far I had come. I was more than 5,000 miles from home, on what could only be described as the trip of a lifetime.

The trip organizer had invited me earlier in the year, but in the throes of a new relationship, I passed on it.

Then, a cycling accident landed me in the emergency room with stitches zigzagging across my face. The morning after the accident, my boyfriend, who had been teaching me to ride and had issued a challenge that led to the accident, compounded the damage. He said he thought we should see less of each other. His words hit me like a slap across my injured face.

When the invitation for the trip came back around after the accident, with the relationship at a dead end, I needed a new adventure. And, frankly, the other side of the world seemed like an appealing place to be at that moment.

I made a quick decision to fly halfway around the globe to meet up with a group of women, most of whom I had never met, to sail around the coast of Turkey. It was not a judgment call; it was a roll of the dice.

Only after we were all together in Turkey would I learn that I was the only "newbie" invited on the trip. The rest of the group not only knew each other, they had much more sailing experience than I did, and they had relationships among them that stretched across the years. It was probably for the best that I was uninformed about this; if I had known, I might have hesitated about joining the trip. And that hesitation would have cost me dearly.

Over the course of ten days of sailing, we had many breathtaking moments, including that morning spent in the spectacular blue grotto. We cruised down the Dalyan River in a boat with a cement hull, topped by beautiful Persian carpets. We also visited the ruins of Kaunos City, which dates from 600 B.C.E., and immersed ourselves in a Turkish mud bath.

We had a few misadventures, like leaving a crew member behind in one port and spending a hilarious evening trying to clear Greek customs in a combination police station/barbershop. We ate and drank delicious local fare in open-air restaurants under moonlit skies.

And we got to know each other.

What a beautiful experience it was for me to be welcomed into

In Uncharted Territory

their fellowship. Women who sail are a breed apart. They have courage, intellect, and an appetite for adventure. They are also a hell of a lot of fun to hang out with.

I arrived for the trip with wounds both physical and emotional. Out beyond the edge of my comfort zone, I found healing and expansion. Buoyed by the embrace of a supportive community, I found the confidence to keep seizing opportunities for adventure that come my way.

I returned home afterward with an armful of memories to hold tight, new friendships to treasure, and a wider perspective on what my life could be. •

Copyright 2024, Alison Rice Bruster

Alison Rice Bruster comes from a long line of women who love the written word. The granddaughter of a librarian, daughter of an English teacher, and sister of a novelist, she was destined to be an avid reader and writer. After a career spent finding the voices of senior business executives, she is writing a new chapter. She holds a BA in English Literature from Queens University of Charlotte and lives in Fort Mill, South Carolina. She is a member of the Charlotte Writers Club, Charlotte Lit, and the North Carolina Writers Network.

Another Door
by Lubrina Burton

I took a deep breath, then opened the door.

Before me, in the spare closet, loomed a Mount Everest-sized pile of out-of-date dresses, a pair of 25-year-old combat boots, and a stack of notebooks and photo albums.

For five years, while I worked on my Army memoir, I ignored this and all the rest of my life's clutter. Later, I promised, after I write, after I edit, then I would face it. But I never got around to it. My book was published last summer, and I spent fall attending book fairs, author readings, and talking with others about their military experiences.

Then Christmas happened. I needed to find decorations, ornaments, and lights. I had no choice but to go into my overstuffed closet. Buried at the bottom was my wreath. I gave it a slight tug. The mountain of clutter grumbled and groaned. I rushed to shut the door, but it was too late. An avalanche spilled out at my feet. The time had come for me to face what I had avoided.

While deciding which items to keep, donate, or discard, I discovered my "Seniors" book filled with keepsakes from my last year of high school. Eager to discover what I thought was worth preserving 25 years ago, I thumbed through the pages. Past a ticket stub to *Titanic*, an 18th birthday card, and a picture of me in Army dress greens was my Senior English project. Written in loopy cursive, the writing portfolio included a family tree, a poem about my mother, and a letter to my father, who I had not seen in a decade. In the letter, I wrote I had completed Basic Training and was soon off to college. I hoped my father would be proud.

I hugged the book to my chest. *Keep.* My eyes watered. *Must be all the dust*, I lied. Reorganizing a single closet, let alone my whole life, seemed too overwhelming. I asked friends for advice. They recommended I read tidying guru Marie Kondo's book. Several years ago, when I watched the TV series, I rolled my eyes as she folded socks and thanked old sweaters. But now, here I was and desperate. So, I checked out the book and promised to keep an open mind.

Instead of focusing on what to toss out, Kondo recommended concentrating on what to keep because it enhances our lives. Only by letting go of that which no longer "sparks joy" will we have space for that which does. Organizing, I realized, was like writing. By editing out what does not contribute, it leaves behind the parts that enhance and strengthen a story. While writing my memoir, I let go of some of my past hurt. I discovered that I, too, was stronger and more open to possibility. By freeing up emotional space, joy crept in to fill the spaces once occupied by pain.

Soon, like a story, my edited home took shape. Reorganizing only confirmed what writing had taught me—I could tackle the messy parts of life I often wished to forget. With that confidence, I applied this skill to my cluttered digital world, starting with unanswered Facebook notifications.

Among the dozens of neglected messages was a year-old friend request from someone I had never met, a woman with my last name — my younger half-sister, my father's youngest daughter. *Nope, delete*, I thought. *You've already closed that door.* But I hesitated, and before I could change my mind again, I hit "accept."

"Hey," I texted. "I guess we're sisters. LOL" I shut my eyes and pressed the send button.

She replied a few moments later, "Hi."

Over several days, we exchanged dozens of text messages. I learned she was a busy wife and a new mom, but still spoke to her parents every day.

Shortly before Christmas she texted, "Mom says you should call Dad."

Sometime soon, I promised myself. *After New Year's.*

On a cold, dark January afternoon, snuggled under a blanket with my pug on my lap, I sat dozing on the couch. A book about carefully choosing what—*whom*—to let into one's life fell from my hands. Nearby, my cellphone buzzed. Half-asleep and bleary-eyed, I squinted to read the screen. A message.

"Dad wants your number."

I put the phone down. *Later, after I sleep, after I clean*, I declared, grumbling to myself. I turned over on the couch, but the text had burned its image onto my brain. Her dad—my dad—wanted to call me. I rolled over again and opened the messenger app. In the reply box, the cursor flashed, awaiting my response. I hovered my thumb over the keyboard. Unsure if I was ready for what might come tumbling out at my feet, I hesitated.

I took a deep breath. •

Copyright 2024, Lubrina Burton

Lubrina Burton lives in Lexington, Kentucky with her husband and pug. She completed the Carnegie Center's Author Academy in 2020 and is now pursuing her MFA at Eastern Kentucky University's Bluegrass Writers Studio. In 2023, Hydra Publications/Erudite Press released her first book, *Shitbag Soldier*, a creative nonfiction memoir detailing her experience as a young soldier in a pre-9/11 U.S. Army. Her short stories and poems are featured in the anthologies, *That Southern Thing, Trouble, Curious Stuff, Twists and Turns, From Pen to Page II*, and *G.I. Days*.

Parallel Universe
by Lynne E Williams

I sprang into action the minute I got the call!

Step 1. Book a flight, the first one available, even if that meant there'd be no time to pack, and I would have to go to the airport with just a purse and the clothes on my back. Actually, that might be better anyway because then I would not be fussing with a carry-on or wasting precious minutes in baggage claim.

Step 2. Rent a car, have it ready and waiting when my flight lands.

Step 3. Drive straight to the hospital, do not pass go, do not stop for coffee, just a quick trip to the restroom on the way to pick up the car.

The only thing that mattered was getting there as quickly as possible. Not to worry about cost, or convenience, or that I was so exhausted I could barely stand up straight.

Not to worry about leaving my 16-month-old son whom I had barely spent a minute apart from since he was born, who was still nursing frequently, who typically only slept for a couple of hours at a time before waking and screaming, wanting to be held and rocked and nursed and sung to.

His father and I were still eyebrow-deep in the first part of the "Nights are long, years are short" adage. Having listened to the false wisdom of unwise friends, family, books, strangers, we were trying so hard to get our sweet innocent boy to sleep in a crib, in his own room. We were fools enough to believe everyone who told us we ought to.

I still don't like to wake up alone in the dark. Why should a tiny person, so new in the world, be ok with it?

The result of our attempt was pure, utter, mind-numbing exhaustion. None of us slept.

That is partly why the first sentence of this story is a big fat lie. Much as I wish that's how things had happened, it is not. When the call came, I froze. I focused on all the wrong things; what to pack, wanting to bring the baby with me, having to pack for him, too. It never even occurred to me that I could just go and trust his father to follow later, with the child I needed and all the things I thought I needed.

Didn't trust him though. Maybe the memory of my last big emergency was still too fresh. A plastic grocery bag stuffed with dozens of washcloths. That's what he brought to the hospital when our son was born and I somehow managed not to die from HELLP syndrome, a complication of severe pre-eclampsia. That strange bag of washcloths had stuck in my mind. I must have assumed he would forget important things or bring all the wrong things. Didn't feel safe leaving the baby with him either. How could he be expected to navigate the airport without me, or to get our son through the trauma of ear-popping take-off and landing without the comfort of my milky breasts to soothe him? What kind of Monster would I be to leave my baby like that?

So, maybe re-writing the story the way I wish it had gone down is supposed to be cathartic. 20/20 hindsight and all that platitudinal crap. Or perhaps there really is a parallel universe in which I actually followed steps, 1, 2, and 3, got to the hospital in plenty of time, and somehow made things different.

In that universe, I held my mother's hand so at least she would not be alone and scared. I ignored the nurse and brought her one last sip of ice-cold Coke, which I know she asked for and was refused.

In that universe, I wiped away the tear before it dried at the edge of her eyelash.

The memory of that salty crystal haunts me.

Maybe, just maybe, there is an alternate reality in which I did not abandon Mom on her deathbed.

###

Trapped on the runway, our flight temporarily grounded by a freak winter storm, waiting for our plane's turn to be de-iced.

Parallel Universe

I'm panicking. Can't breathe, can't be still: My toddler son squirms on my lap, perhaps feeling the fear and grief that course through me in waves of guilty despair. His father reaches for him, but I won't relinquish the solid, grounding warmth of his little body.

A kind flight attendant tries to soothe me. I cannot be comforted.

LET ME OFF THIS PLANE I NEED TO GET TO HER NOW! I imagine that I'm screaming. It comes out a wordless whimper.

Then, a sudden calm, an invisible cloak. A breath, a breeze, a knowing. I no longer have a reason to hurry. It is already too late.

My mother is gone. •

Copyright 2024, Lynne E Williams

Emerging author Lynne E Williams is a native New Englander who lives in Charlotte, North Carolina, with her two cats, two dogs, two teenaged sons and their father. Lynne is a graduate of Clark University in Worcester, MA where she double majored in Music and Theater instead of English but was nevertheless named a Writing Fellow of the University. She is a member of the Charlotte Writer's Club and Charlotte Lit, and a two-time finalist in CWC's nonfiction contest. Her story "The Power Drill" was included in the fall 2022 PSPP anthology *Twists and Turns*.

Marsh Riches
by Ginny Foard

The marsh sticks up scrappily towards the sky. The grasses are yellow. Or green. Or muddy brown. They mix together. They push into thick sideways piles. Water slides up and around the stalks as the tides rise high. The receding tides pull hard against the grassy roots with loud burbling slops.

I am the sturdy jogger plodding along the marsh edge. The wren wobbling on top of a grassy spike watches from a safe distance. Skinny legs of great white egrets lift up daintily out of the sucking, stinking pluff mud, while the birds' alert eyes and ready beaks swivel above their tall towers of white featheriness. *Splash!* lands the pelican, with webby feet splayed wide.

I, the sturdy jogger, plod along. On the footpath, flattened remains of a raccoon decay where a passing car's velocity tossed them. A turkey vulture watches for another chance to access this booty when the coast is clear. A long slimy cylinder slithers into the thickness of the marsh almost too fast to be seen.

I, sturdy, plod along. A big blue sky lifts up from the mostly flat horizon ahead, to the left, to the right. Wind sweeps across from the left. It crosses from the ocean, over a narrow sandy island, over expansive marshes, over the two-lane causeway and its parallel footpath, into the scrappy marshes spreading forever to the right of the footpath.

I, sturdy, plod. Ahead on the path, against the crosswind, a man and his dog. Small silhouettes at first. They make their way towards me. His jacket flaps. The dog's leash swings towards the marsh. We all grow larger, slowly.

I plod. No stopping. My goal today is to jog there and back again. No walking. Forward. Road on the left, marsh on the right, windy sky ahead. Plod, plod, plod.

I jog to the right on the footpath. The man and his dog are nearing on the left. We each have our own pace, leaning sideways against the wind that pushes us towards the scrubby, sucky, stinky marsh. Jackets flap. The leash swings.

A car barrels towards us. White, a new-model four-door sedan. It's alone on the road. Fast. Windows down. The wind whips through it, inside and out. As the car gets closer, its radio spills into the quiet marshy wind.

Then the car's almost beside us, the footpath souls. A shout bursts from the car, while a hand reaches out the passenger's window and arches onto the roof.

Leftover beach energy, I speculate as I plod forward. No stopping.

Suddenly flying papers fill the air, streaming from above the car's roof, blowing onto the footpath, sticking in the grasses, tumbling into the marsh edges. I see them scattering out in front of me, focus on my forward efforts, plod, plod, towards all that litter tumbling on the ground ahead.

The man and his dog also take notice. The man swings his head up, over towards the road where the car is almost lost to visibility now, where the passenger's arm had just released wads of papers into our windy path. His dog eyes the scene, puzzled at the interrupted routine.

The man begins picking up all he can. Most is on the footpath and its edges, only a few are beyond reach in the marsh.

As I plod closer, the litter begins to look like money. Green bills. Monopoly money? Then, closer, it's real dollar bills. Thick on the ground. Blown and tugged by the wind, heading into the marsh soon.

Forward, no stopping. The man picks up fistfuls of bills, filling his pockets. He's in a whirlwind of green. "THIS IS CRAZY," he shouts as I plod by, "I won't forget this day!"

"Fantastic," I say, plodding along. No stopping. *He'll clean it up*, I tell myself.

A few yards further, I see ahead yet more untamed bills waving in the grass tops. A few have fallen off the path into the sloping edges of the marsh. I glance behind to see the man busily gathering bills as he walks away from me on the path.

Marsh Riches

The wind pushes the bills. They will not wait for the man. These bills are headed for the marsh.

Now or never, I realize. I jettison my "no stopping" plan. I bend to gather bills, stepping down into the marsh edges to collect the ones that I can reach before they blow into the wetlands.

A few minutes later, the man and his dog approach. "What a day," he chuckles, "here, take this." He pulls his fist from a pocket, full of a wad of bills.

"No, thanks, I've got some here," I say as I show him my collected wad.

We laugh together. •

Copyright 2024, Ginny Foard

Growing up in the South means hearing and sharing stories. Ginny Foard learned a lot that way and keeps on trying to find out more about it all. The air is thick with good stories. She lives in a little post office box on Sullivans Island, South Carolina.

What We Do
by David Inserra

My cousin Paul and I worked our way up from the floor of the canyon, slowly, through the intense heat, to the rest cabin only a quarter of a mile of trail below the south rim. The stifling air in the small room held ten sweaty bodies packed tightly on the benches stretched alongside the walls. Each hiker privately hoped to complete the arduous climb so they could have a story to tell. We too had a story to tell, and we hoped that the ranger would listen.

Leaning against the back wall, I spoke into the receiver of the emergency phone. "You don't understand," I said. "No. Her brothers wanted to race to the Colorado River … She told them she couldn't make it, so they left her at the bottom."

This phone call was not going anywhere. The ranger half-listened to our tale only responding with an infrequent grunt or the occasional *uh-huh*.

Three hours before, Paul and I sat at Plateau Point and enjoyed our lunches. We dangled our feet over the edge of the cliff, and we marveled at the raging Colorado River 1500 feet below us. We enjoyed watching eagles and hawks glide along the wind currents. The surrounding desert held other hikers, deer, snakes, and rabbits. All making this a memorable experience.

The ranger asked me to tell him again about the girl who needed assistance. "She hiked into the canyon wearing sandals," I said. "She didn't bring any water or any snacks with her." I let out a frustrated sigh at the ranger's lack of concern.

Exhausted eyes from the other hikers in the cabin watched me with interest.

"I told you we don't know her. She met a group of hikers from New York, and they walked together for a while. My cousin and I joined up with them. Shortly afterward, the girl passed out. We doused her with water and that brought her around, but then she turned blue and started throwing up. We need someone to go down and help her."

When you stand on the south rim of the canyon it is easy to get lost in the myriad colors painted across the vibrant landscape. Reds. Greens. Purples. Blues. Browns. Dramatic vistas as far as the eye can see, all etched into the sand and stone, carved over the centuries by the Colorado River. Research before the trip told us that when we stood on the south rim the temperature could be 75 degrees. At the same time, the temperature on the floor of the canyon could be 110 degrees. So, we came prepared. I purchased new hiking boots and a backpack. We brought extra water, snacks, sandwiches, and plenty of sunblock. Paul and I were going to take the week to hike the canyon and explore the surrounding area. Right now, the idea of spending more time tramping this treacherous yet beautiful terrain was the farthest thing from our minds.

I paced as far as the cord on the emergency phone would let me. I tried to make myself clear to the ranger, I tried to make him understand what was happening. This girl, this teenager, was in trouble. The group of women from New York were staying with her at the bottom of the canyon while Paul and I climbed to the rest cabin, to seek assistance.

A fat man sitting across from me poked his hiking partner in the stomach and rolled his eyes. They both shared a private laugh. Across from him, a rail thin woman, wearing tights and a loose-fitting top, shook her head as if she knew what was coming.

When I hung up the phone, Paul stepped close. "What did the ranger say?"

I pointed to the spigot on the opposite wall of the cramped cabin. "He told us to fill our water bottles and go back down."

Paul repeated in disbelief, "Go back down?"

When I nodded, Paul and I shared an unspoken understanding regarding the task ahead of us.

"Okay." My cousin shrugged.

As we filled our water bottles a voice called through the cabin. "You're not seriously going back." The fat man's pudgy hand wiped his sweaty brow.

What We Do

Another hiker called, "You guys are crazy. You don't even know them."

Someone else snapped, "Why don't you guys just get out of here. You'll never see them again."

Our bodies ached. We were sweaty and tired. We were a quarter mile from the Bright Angel trailhead. It would have been so easy to continue up and out to safety, back to our own little lives. But there was never any doubt.

"We're going back," I said. "It's what we do."

As Paul and I walked toward the exit, one hiker started to clap. Then another. Then everyone joined in. The clapping continued until we were gone. •

Copyright 2024, David Inserra

David Inserra lives on Hilton Head Island, South Carolina with his wife Ellen Titus and their dog, Mindy. David's most recent work appears in the PSPP release, Sooner or Later. He is a member of the Island Writers Network and works at the local Unitarian Church. David's first novel, a speculative thriller titled "In Your Own Backyard," is currently being queried to agents. He is also a musician who has written over 400 songs, most being about his wife. Visit davidinserra.weebly.com.

Getting a Head Start
by Arlene Mandell

Gone!

In one fell swoop, my rosy future had nosedived into nothingness. Four years at New York University, Greenwich Village; degree in Early Childhood Education; New York City teaching license—all gone.

Adding to the debacle, I had to call Dad to come get me and my belongings. I was renting a minuscule, windowless, furnished room at a facility for working women in Mid-Manhattan near my first teaching assignment. The room was horrid, dim, and dreary but my paragon of independence! "I won't tell Mother how you're living," Dad sympathized. *Thank God for small mercies.* We drove to my parents' home north of Manhattan, in the suburban Bronx.

As a teacher, I wanted to introduce children to the school experience by making learning fun. Burrowing through creative ideas at the NYU library produced a jam-packed binder of activities. My student-teaching kindergarten placements all went smoothly. This was my niche!

Unfortunately, I was assigned to fifth grade—not my strong suit. Chaos reigned! The principal, after repeatedly taking over, transferred me to second grade; but—same problem. *Humiliation. Devastation. The only way out was resignation.* It meant losing my coveted license. I had no choice.

At my parents' home, a paralytic malaise engulfed me, immobilizing my limbs. Doctors did not understand. I did; it was my life imploding. Depressive episodes were familiar to me, but none this bad. Experience cautioned: Take action! Quickly! Or freefall into a chasm I could *never* climb out of.

I pulled myself together enough to contact my college mentor. Stunned, he encouraged me to get a substitute-teacher's license ASAP. The pay scale was less, but I qualified and could still teach. Having a plan super-energized me. Acquiring that license, I visited every grade school in my parents' area, offering to substitute—with one caveat: kindergarten only! At the peep of day, I was ready to roll, guitar at the front door. Calls (and callbacks!) poured in all year long, rebuilding my confidence.

That summer, in an unprecedented move, city newspapers listed available teaching positions. A Head Start program was opening in a public school on Cherry Street, way south of Lower Manhattan. I arranged an interview. Landing that job would be a practical reason to move back into the city.

With a generous welcome, the principal described the Head Start format: 15 pre-kindergartners each, in morning and afternoon sessions, with two full-time assistants from the community. Home visits to every child's family, by me, were required, plus monthly workshops in my classroom for parents only. Teachers new to Head Start would attend orientation. My excitement was contagious; I was hired on the spot.

Relieved and happy, I reconnoitered the neighborhood. It was noon; a scrumptious smell drew me into a corner *bodega*. Locals were eating *cuchifritos* and sipping *Café Bustelo* espresso coffee. I ordered both—new flavors to someone who grew up on bagels in the Bronx. The meal was delicious, the people friendly. *I'm going to like it here*, I mused.

By the end of August, as I prepared my classroom, the two assistants, Hilda and Lettie arrived, introducing themselves. Their bilingual skills would prove invaluable at my monthly workshops in recruiting parents to participate in field trips, holiday parties, and home visits from Max, our classroom pet guinea pig. Involving parents in school life was a critical element of the Head Start program!

On the first morning of school, I gathered my little 4-year-olds in a circle to sing. All eyes were glued on the guitar I strummed, energetically. All, except Patricia—joyless, unresponsive, eyes cast downward. Later, while other children bustled about exploring the room, she opened the big paste jar and gobbled a mouthful. She was hungry, she whimpered.

From then on, I had food ready for her the minute she arrived. I had hugs and kisses for her, too, and lots of them; none of the children asked why. Given time and a satisfied tummy, she tackled the puzzles, cuddled the guinea pig, learned to print her name on paintings to take home.

Late December, Patricia came to school all dressed up in bright-blue taffeta and red barrettes, beaming like someone with a happy secret. Enveloping her in a bear hug, I asked why she looked so special that day. That precious, little-girl-face looked straight up at mine, barely pushing the words out half-whispered, "Because you like me." The most endearing moment among multitudes to follow.

That year proved exceptional: Patricia learned school was fun; my parent workshops grew steadily, from just three curious moms at first, to full capacity; Hilda and Lettie were proud guests at my wedding in June to Mr. Mandell, the sixth-grade teacher; and I had found my true calling.

Daring to take one small step forward in my personal life had illuminated a pathway enabling me to give my students their own head start forward to climb, rise, soar towards a promising future. •

Copyright 2024, Arlene Mandell

Arlene Mandell is an artist living in Linville, North Carolina, proudly celebrating her 11th year at Carlton Gallery in Banner Elk. (carlton-gallery.com/arlene-mandell). A native New Yorker, relocating to the Blue Ridge Mountains with Captain Dan ignited a passion to write. Her "6-minute Stories" podcasts include: "Eye of the Dolphin," "Artist Borne," "Gobsmacked in the Gulfstream," "Renegade Daughter," "It Started with a Typo," "Shopping for the Homeless," "Thirteen Candles in the Dark," "The Promise of Romance," "At 5 and 95, Mother Was a Star," "In the Heart of Trauma," and "The Jig Is Up."

A Father's Dream
by Thomas Gery

Relationships and war are both uncertain, yet both require decisions.

1967 was a tumultuous time in America. Personally, I was feeling lost: college life; part time work to survive living on my own; far away from the loving cocoon of family; pressure to conform.

I was caught between my desire and my father's expectation. Dad always anticipated my earning a college degree. He was a high school drop out with a touch of juvenile delinquency: an intelligent man with undiagnosed dyslexia who grew up in a well-off, white-collar family. The WW II Navy set him straight; he went on to be a skilled brick mason. My father wanted better for his first-born son.

I was predestined. The high school college prep curriculum led to junior college enrollment. In the third semester, Dad's plan for me went awry. I wanted to quit school. It meant shattering father's vision. Would my dropping out resurrect Dad's personal nightmare of being a failure in the eyes of his parents?

My parents and three siblings were a thousand miles away. I felt a sense of loyalty to them, particularly Dad. Deeper still was fear of condemnation. I sought an honorable alternative. I made the choice alone.

The Government conscripted almost 2 million citizens during the Vietnam War. In 1968 I was sworn into the US Army along with nearly 300,000 other men. I had a student deferment but requested the local draft board reclassify me to 1-A. I was not dropping out; I was going in. How could a war-time veteran see my action as anything but honorable? The 19-year-old son was playing it safe, heedless of the danger. Now a father myself, I understand the dread and terror my parents felt.

I completed the third semester, returning home for the Christmas holidays after final exams. In early January, I reported for the trip to Fort Benning, in Georgia. My ploy to avoid parental criticism worked; Dad knew my oath to the Constitution was irrevocable. He had the grace to put aside ill will at seeing his own dream thwarted. He wished me well, his love expressed with a long hug and tearful goodbye. He foresaw better than I the peril ahead. During my year in Vietnam, on average, 17 Americans died daily. The night before deployment I heard the depth of my father's anguish.

Joanne, a smart engaging young woman, and I had developed a relationship. When together it was magical. We were inseparable during my leave from the Army. The last evening at home we were with a group at her friend's house. Joanne planned for us to be alone. It was emotional. We kissed with adolescent passion. Our embrace intense, our bodies becoming one with unfathomable pleasure. The evening felt like a movie scene. We were at the threshold of separation: she, at home completing high school, me, the kid-soldier off to war.

Joanne's parents approved our dating, hanging out, doing young adult things but with limits. She had a curfew. On that last night we blew through it. Joanne was ready for parental consequences.

A short time later as dawn approached, I reflected on the recent few hours of ecstasy and tears while imagining a frightening year of unknowns. The kitchen wall phone rang. An irate father demanded to speak to Dad.

Shaking off sleep, Dad took the phone, said hello, then listened. Joanne's parent blasted away with fatherly indignation defending his daughter's honor, denouncing my conduct. In response, Dad respectfully delivered a few words in somber, measured tone, "My son leaves for Vietnam tomorrow. How do you think I feel?"

I came home from war to fulfill my father's expectations. He saw me twice in cap and gown, then followed my career in social work. I often expressed appreciation for his influence. When visiting our family he asked about my work, a flicker of pride crossing his face. His two grandchildren elicited a greater glow of joy and love.

In 2010, Dad's life was ebbing. Shortly before he died, I assembled the family before an emotional flight south. Physically miserable with a belly bloated from fluid overload, his spirits soared during our visit. The recent portrait of my beautiful wife, our children, their partners, two adorable great-grandbabies was his last vision. He had achieved a father's dream: his son did better. Dad was leaving as I had over 40 years earlier. This time there was no uncertainty about return; we knew. I hugged his weakening body one last time, whispering through tears of grief, "Thank you Dad, I love you." •

Copyright 2024, Thomas Gery

Thomas Gery, a common man with uncommon experiences lives in Berks County, Pennsylvania. He served in the U.S. Army with duty in Vietnam. As a social worker he helped children, youth, and adults in a variety of practice venues and situations throughout a work life of 40 years. Married with two adult children and two grandchildren, he is currently writing his life's story to provide answers to questions his kids will never ask. His first two published stories appeared in Personal Story Publishing Project—*Lost & Found*, spring 2023 and *Sooner or Later*, fall 2023.

Fit To Be Tied
by S.G. Benson

In a box of newspaper clippings, I recently found an old article with my byline. It began: "Move over, Alps and Rockies! The mountains aren't the only place ice climbers can find a challenge. Cold springs, seeping from the sheer cliffs that flank the Niobrara River near Valentine, freeze solid in mid-winter, creating scalable ice cascades. Last weekend, visitors thronged the Niobrara Ice Jam, Nebraska's ice climbers' jamboree."

The article described two Colorado adventurers who trekked to neighboring Nebraska to see what icy challenges the prairie state offers.

Most people, including me, don't equate Nebraska with world-class ice climbing. So, as a newspaper correspondent for the *Daily News*, I felt surprised when my editor asked me to cover the event. It proved to be a chilling experience—pun intended.

A cardinal rule of journalism is that reporters should never appear in their own articles, never be the story. Now, years later, I can share what happened behind the scenes.

I arrived at the parking area to find a dozen climbers checking their gear. They wore crampons (metal spikes) strapped to their boots to keep them from slipping. I did not.

The group planned to hike to the precipice, secure their ropes to trees, and rappel to the base of the ice cliff, where they would test several new, uncharted, routes as they climbed back to the top. I intended to remain topside, using that vantage point to follow the action.

As the trek began, I immediately lagged behind, slipping and sliding on the ice. The hikers soon disappeared from my sight. Two men brought up the rear of our caravan of climbers: a magazine photographer from Lincoln and my friend Stuart, a local park ranger. They slowed to accompany me, occasionally reaching out a steadying hand as I scrambled on the slick trail. They both wore proper footwear.

Prairie yielded to pine forest as we neared the bluff. The trail began descending slightly, and it became nearly impossible to keep my feet under me. Right at the edge of the chasm, I lost my balance and teetered on the brink, staring at sharp rocks lining the river a hundred feet below. Stuart grabbed me just in time.

Terrified, I considered returning home without my story. *If I go, they'll never give me another plum assignment.* I looked at Stuart.

"You're not gonna like this," he said, "but it will keep you safe and free both of your hands to write and to shoot pictures." He took a stout rope from his equipment belt and tied me securely to a sturdy pine.

The men pulled their climbing gear from their packs, tied
a rope to another large tree, and waved goodbye to me before
rappelling over the edge.

Leaning over the lip of the precipice, I used both hands
to photograph and jot notes as I watched the climbers below
for the next couple of hours. With the temperature in the
upper teens, my ungloved writing hand soon became numb.
My parka felt inadequate, and my feet gradually lost feeling.
It occurred to me that if my benefactors were unable to climb
back up the ice wall, I might be in a desperate situation.

Daylight began to fade. I capped my camera lens and pocketed
my notebook. Peering again over the edge, I gasped when
I saw nobody below. The climbers' voices that had earlier filled
the afternoon had disappeared. Hearing only the wind and my
own heartbeat punctuated my isolation, and the thought
of being entirely alone terrified me. *Where did they all go?*

I twisted in my bindings and strained towards the knot
in Stuart's rope. It was just beyond the tips of my fingers.
I don't even have a pocketknife, I thought. *Now what?*

The shadows deepened along the river and the rocks below;
the chill in the air sharpened.

How long before someone notices me missing? Would anyone—at all?

As my anxiety rose, a rustling sound broke into my consciousness. I looked around but saw no one. *What is that noise?*

A sudden movement drew my eyes to the ground several yards

away. Stuart's rappelling rope, still tied to a tree, moved slightly, making tiny sounds against the ice. I craned my neck to look over the rim but spotted nothing. Still, I could hear what sounded like faint, heavy breathing.

The rope moved again, more this time. A few minutes later, Stuart's head popped up from under the cliff edge.
He grinned.

"Did you think we forgot you?"

Hoisting himself onto the top, he reached back and pulled up the photographer after him.

My story ran a few days later. My editor said the readers loved it.

If only he knew, I thought. If only *they* knew.

I refolded the yellowed newspaper clipping and slipped it back into the box, grateful I had not become a footnote to *another* story—my obituary. •

Copyright 2024, S.G. Benson

S. G. (Sandy) Benson lives in Warne, North Carolina, where she is a member of the North Carolina Writers Network-West. Her work has appeared in numerous magazines and newspapers and received awards from the Nebraska Press Women. She published her first book in 2021, *My Mother's Keeper: One Family's Journey Through Dementia.* Her next book, *Dear Folks: Letters Home from World War II, 1943-1946* is scheduled for release in April 2024. Details at https://www.sandygbenson.com/

The Time Had Come
by Ellen Zaroff

I had been working in the service industry with people who were alternately wonderful and appreciative or nasty and entitled. It's more often the former group I dealt with but of course it would always be the latter group who would ruin the day. Such is the nature of hotels, health spas and people in general, especially when focused on their leisure.

I lived in a two-story walk-up, having been ejected from my lovely, albeit roach-infested apartment, due to a technicality in the lease; the technicality being, I wasn't on it.

After expressing my indignation, I found a "one bedroom" which was a studio with a partial door down the middle. It was above a small but very potent Indian restaurant where the aroma of curry wafted up the stairs and under my not-insulated door. I like the smell of curry but like anything one is inundated with, it went from pleasant to overwhelming to unnoticeable. I thought it was gone but my friends never failed to ask if someone had ordered curry when we were out to dinner. The apartment had a reversal on the trope of no hot water -- having only hot water -- which meant getting clean was a game of dodging in and out of the shower's boiling stream and I came to envy the units with a bathtub in the kitchen, which could be filled and left to cool.

After Little India's wait staff had long gone, the night girls came out to ply their trade, walking the street or chatting with each other on the corner. If I was returning from the shift which ran late, they would invite me to join them, laughing that they probably made more in a night than I did in a week, and they were not likely wrong. While the night held camaraderie and playfulness, the morning held fatigue and looking worse-for-wear as they boarded the bus or subway to take up what the rest of us considered a 'normal' life of kids, laundry, groceries and whatever else we all do in our daily routines.

I had a friend Ginger who worked for a major hotelier with properties in exotic places, exotic being anywhere but the cold Northeast. She invited me, on several occasions, to give her a call and she would get me a position somewhere warm, doing something fun. I told her I was working on my plan, which included staying in the grey winters and sweltering summers but was building toward a bigger picture, the images of which were still somewhat fuzzy.

I came home one night, exhausted. The last customers had refused to leave long after it was evident that the place was closing. We finally got on the speaker to advise that the guard dogs were soon being released to act as security during the night. Human feet quickly padded toward the door, and we locked up, chuckling to ourselves. If there weren't repercussions, there would be another group, another night, when we would have to use the same tactic.

It suddenly felt like I was chasing my tail.

I was tired.

I was lonely.

My job, with its odd hours, prevented regular social interactions with people who worked a 9-to-5 day.

Winter was approaching and the girls on the corner had changed. The gentle teasing on my walk home was replaced with suspicious looks over shoulders, and backs turned my way.

To cheer myself up the next day, I thought I would take a shopping trip to a fancy store, despite that I did not enjoy shopping nor was I in the habit of spending money on clothes. After a short half hour, I found myself outside, my back to the door, watching a drizzle of thin rain quickly turn into heavier drops which seemed to come from all angles. I stood there until the lights began to come on and the people on the sidewalk changed from women tugging at bags or small children, to folks in suits carrying briefcases or newspapers tucked under their arms, still unread from the morning's purchase.

And still I stood there, not wanting to go into the wet or to my empty street, with only passing customers buying tandoori to take-away. I stood there not wanting to go home, not wanting to stay in the doorway, unsure of what the next few minutes might hold. I wondered if this was how a mental breakdown might begin.

It seemed likely.

It was then I knew.

It was then I decided the time to leap had come. If I waited a few hours or days, those would turn into weeks or months, and the moment and its urgency would be lost.

I dialed Ginger.

When she picked up, I said, "Please, send me away, somewhere, anywhere." •

Copyright 2024, Ellen Zaroff

Ellen Zaroff lives in New York City and has recently published three books: *A Layered Tress*, *A Tree's Tale*, and *Once, Upon Reflection*. Her fourth book is due out soon. She runs a small foundation and travels trying to help community projects while collecting stories and sharing stories from around the world.

This story involves a suicide.

A Lost Curmudgeon
by Akira Odani

I received a cryptic email message from my friend George one summer morning:

"Crossing with Charon tomorrow. Look for me when you get to the other side. Vale."

To me, its tone suggested finality even though I wasn't familiar with Charon or Vale. Weeks before, he whispered over coffee he might exit from the world soon, in a voice like a soldier in a POW camp—tired, resigned, spent. I surmised later George had sunk into an existential crisis.

Should I call him? Is he asking for help? I wondered. I was busy, needing to pack for a ten-day trip to upstate New York. I hesitated. I did not call. Now, I question why. Was I afraid? What could I say to dissuade him?

A few days later, while checking emails I received the news: George killed himself. *Oh! No!*

Energy drained from my spine. I slumped down to the floor. I was devastated and felt responsible somehow. I later confirmed that Charon was the mythological ferryman into the underworld. Vale meant "farewell" in Latin.

George was not a bosom buddy. We didn't go fishing, bar hopping, or traveling together, but we were more than acquaintances. I enjoyed his wicked sarcasm about corrupt politicians, mass ignorance, and uneducated youth—their inability to speak or read, their drab clothing, and tattooed bare skins, in his assessments. George was a curmudgeon—irascible, cantankerous, and stubborn about his ideas, even the wild ones. Still, he was widely read on the classics, foreign literature, history, and current affairs. The problem with George, however, was that he also subscribed to some fringe publications and harbored outrageous conspiracy theories, such as some relating to the Twin Towers' collapse on 9/11 and the JFK assassination.

George did, however, encourage me to write widely, creatively, and even about fantastic plots. I felt a kinship with him. He lived in the universe of Latin and Greek philosophers, especially the Stoics. He published several books on the subject. One thick volume he gave me contained writings from Homer, Socrates, Cicero, Seneca, and many others. George was a learned fellow.

I searched for a clue in that book that might explain his suicide. Epictetus, a Stoic, penned: "He who cannot be bought by pleasure, or pain, or reputation, or wealth, can when it seems good to him, destroy himself in front of the tyrant and leave this world; whose slave can you call him? Who rules him other than himself?" George was not a slave to anybody, but perhaps he had taken the hypothetical analogy too literally.

George and I met on occasion at a local coffee shop in the outdated style of men's confabulation. I invited another friend, Ian, a widely traveled, wise fellow, to join us. We converged bi-weekly to discuss whatever came to our minds. We often disagreed. George was the opposite of Ian, a firebrand liberal. George cast his recent vote simply based on a candidate's distaste for government, politics, and politicians. Ian and I focused on the positive aspects of liberalism and democracy while admitting their limitations. George despaired while we hoped. That was the crucial difference.

One afternoon, George argued that slavery was not a shameful chapter of American history. Slavery, he said, existed and thrived in Europe and in Africa for centuries as an element of cross-border trade. That argument infuriated Ian. Tensions rose, and then George poured gasoline onto a smoldering fire, bringing another incendiary theory questioning the horrors wrought by Nazi Germany.

Ian vaulted, "That's it, bastard! I can no longer sit here. You are such a foolish man!" Ian's eyes glared, and his face reddened; he rushed out the door.

George's worldview was bleak. He was a bachelor, living alone, while Ian was happily married, and I lived with a committed partner. His lack of an intimate partner might have contributed to his lonesome alienation from the world. I agreed with many of his critical views of humanity, minus his conspiracy theories. Unlike him, however, I enjoy being alive, smelling the aroma of fresh coffee in the morning, strolling the beach, gazing at the golden moon in the night sky, observing flowers

A Lost Curmudgeon

bloom, and hearing cardinals chirping and children laughing in a schoolyard. Life's pleasures are more abundant than its disappointments.

I miss George. Thinking back over my conversations with him, I feel our relationship was cut short. And, perhaps I could have been more proactive and invited him into my tangible, not solely intellectual world—hiking the shores and woods, appreciating changing seasons, and listening to children and birds singing. That might have been my gift to him. But George left me with a final gift—helping me realize that our small pleasures on earth are plentiful and certainly worthy of our time.

It is too late to thank him now, perhaps on the other side.

Vale. •

Editor's Note: The author uses pseudonyms to protect privacy.

Copyright 2024, Akira Odani

Akira Odani lives in the ancient city of St. Augustine, Florida. He belongs to Taste Life Twice Writers and the Florida Writers Association. Born in Tokyo, he had written extensively for the Japanese media. Still, more recently, his interest has turned to writing in English and subjects related to his experiences interacting with the two cultures. Some of his work has appeared in the pages of FWA anthologies, *The Weekly Avocet*, and PSPP's *Twists and Turns*, *Lost & Found*, and *Sooner or Later*. He stays active, meditating, swimming, and playing pickleball.

Perish the Thought
by Kenneth Chamlee

In a seven-month span over my sabbatical year of 2007-2008, two *go-now* or likely *never-go* opportunities opened for me. Each trip was far from home and left disparate impressions, leading to a sober realization.

In January of 2008, I was selected for an intercollegiate field trip to the Galapagos Islands sponsored by the Appalachian College Association. Sixteen faculty from 13 schools toured the archipelago on a small boat, eating and sleeping onboard and arriving at a new island each morning. We were there to experience a "living classroom" and to return with a unique environmental awareness. On Española, our walk at the Punta Suarez visitor site stunned me with its amplitude of life.

Marine iguanas clustered everywhere, their coal-black skin grained like leather but with feet and claws of shiny scales. A spiky crest topped each head, like a comb with broken teeth, and they frequently snorted salt out of nostrils set in grim, prehistoric faces.

Birds unseen in North America evidenced every phase of their lives. Blue-footed booby pairs step-danced their mating ritual, each slowly lifting one foot, then the other. Spreading wings high and pointing bills straight up, males whistled, and females honked as they circled. Just feet away, females sat on eggs in shallow, guano-splattered sand-scrapes serving as nests. Recently born chicks were ugly, featherless knobs of rough skin and stubby wings. In other nests, older nestlings had grown into fuzzy misshapen bodies as lumpy as a child's project made with cotton balls.

Our group and our guide Antonio were the only human beings in this place. We walked slowly, stepping around the oblivious birds, quietly observing and photographing the astounding diversity at our feet and in the air above. Just offshore, four other craft awaited their turns to disembark. The number of visits and visitors, plus the timing and pacing of each group, is strictly controlled by the government of Ecuador and Galapagos National Park and Marine Reserve. It is the only way to preserve the biotic integrity of each island and landing site. By limiting tourist exposure and forbidding interaction, the boobies and oystercatchers don't fear people. They are not tame but unconditioned to threat. How different that two-hour excursion felt from another tour just months earlier.

The previous June, after teaching a three-week course in British Literature in London for the International Enrichment program, I extended my stay abroad to join a tour of Italy. I was already in Europe, the start date coincided with the end of my term, and the concurrence seemed fortuitous.

When our tour reached Rome, we had a day scheduled to see the Vatican. I was awestruck by the vastness and splendor inside Saint Peter's Basilica. But my group was one of dozens shambling through the Gallery of Maps and Tapestry Hall to an incessant babel, then down long corridors filled with busts, urns, and hundreds of exquisitely ornamented ceiling paintings.

Crowds of people moving *en masse* were pressed forward by those coming behind, with no time to stop and admire the sculptures or the artistry above. I was able to follow our guide Barbara only by spotting her red unopened umbrella jabbed above the hubbub. I could not hear any of her commentary over the surge of voices, scuffling feet, and the clatter of cameras and backpacks.

After twisting down some narrow staircases we were suddenly in the Sistine Chapel, dimly lit for protection of the art. Every second I looked up to admire the glorious vault I either bumped into somebody or somebody bumped into me. Instead of a respectful hush, the swell of noise increased as people could neither contain excitement nor master their manners. Every minute or two a voice on the P.A. begged ironically *"Quiet, please. This is a sacred space. Please, no photography."* And for 10 seconds there would be a lull, then the cacophonous drone and flash bursts resumed.

Being in the presence of Michaelangelo's masterpiece, an experience I had greatly anticipated, was profoundly disappointing. Volumes of visitors were chuted through this venerated chamber—numbers being profit—with the quality of encounter secondary or even irrelevant.

These two diametrically opposed instances exemplified to me how differently institutions and the public can view protection and privilege. I felt exceptionally fortunate to have visited each site, but thought, what if authorities in Ecuador allowed Basilica-like crowds to swarm the Galapagos? And did officials at the Vatican not consider the hordes' deteriorating effects of dust, mass exhalation and vibrations on their treasures? I had my two rare chances, but without vigilant supervisory discretion and accountability, the *now* of today's beauties and wonders could easily become the *no more* of tomorrow. •

Copyright 2024, Kenneth Chamlee

Kenneth Chamlee's work has appeared in six previous Personal Story Publishing Project anthologies. His latest collections are *If Not These Things* (Kelsay Books, 2022) and *The Best Material for the Artist in the World*, a poetic biography of 19th-century American landscape painter Albert Bierstadt (Stephen F. Austin State University Press, 2023). Ken lives in Mills River, North Carolina, and is an active member of the North Carolina Poetry Society and the North Carolina Writers' Network. Learn more at www.kennethchamlee.com.

Buck
by M. J. Norwood

Baseball brings out the kid in me. I learned everything I know about baseball from my dad. Always willing to pitch to me, while I waved around an old bat, his words of encouragement lingered. "Keep your eyes on the ball. Tighten your grip." I listened attentively, but there were few baseball teams for girls in the 1970s. I was content to watch baseball on TV, and I envied fans lucky enough to catch baseballs.

We loved the Atlanta Braves. The Turner Broadcasting System brought them into homes around the nation from 1977 until 2007. I remember sitting by my dad, watching many of those games throughout the 1980s. The announcers were as much a part of the game as the players.

"Hello, I'm Skip Caray…" "…and I'm Pete Van Wieren." For the next three hours they called every play, and my dad and I watched it all.

I went to college and eventually moved away, but continued to support the Braves, and watch those games. I knew my dad was watching, too.

Buck

During one game towards the end of the 1985 season, Skip was speaking about a catcher, recently brought up from the minors.

"Larry Owen," Skip announced with enthusiasm. "Buck," he chuckled. Pete laughed, as well. "The other players call him Buck." *Buck?* Hmm. Oh! Could it be Buck Owen, like the name of country music legend, Buck Owens? Larry "Buck" Owen. I smiled. During the seventh inning stretch, my dad called, and asked me if I wanted to go to a game with him. A game? In Atlanta? He offered to buy the tickets. "I'll drive!" I said.

So, at age 22, I attended my first Major League Baseball game at Atlanta-Fulton County Stadium. Hot dogs, draft beer, red dirt infield, bright white lines, green grassy outfield, and the realization that I was breathing the same air as my heroes. Dale Murphy, Bob Horner, Rafael Ramirez, and Bruce Benedict, had me floating like the Good Year Blimp. We found our seats, which were a few rows above the bullpen.

Several players were warming up on the field. I noticed a small group of fans gathered at the bottom of the steps behind the railing and I opened my program to find the box score. I heard someone say, "That was nice. They're not supposed to do that." I glanced at the small group and saw a child holding up a baseball. Was there a chance that one of those players might toss me a ball? It would never happen with me sitting here. I had to be close. My dad handed me his glove as I stood up and made my way towards the rail.

I towered above the small cluster of children, who were shouting at the players, and being ignored. "Hey! Mister! Throw me a ball! Hey! Mister!" over and over.

Who were those players closest to us? "Cerone," I read on the back of a jersey. I knew he was one of the catchers. *Who was the other guy?* "Owen." Oh yes, Larry Owen, the catcher called up from the minors. *What did his teammates call him? Buck?* It was Buck, Buck Owen.

"Buck!" I called. "Hey, Buck!" I shouted. His head whipped sharply towards me. I held up my gloved left hand and, much to my astonishment, he threw a baseball in my direction. It was a bit high, so I had to jump. I reached up as far as I could, and *THWUMP*. That ball landed safely in my glove. The youngsters looked up at me in awe. *Should I keep the ball?* So many deserving young fans. I could be their hero. Make someone's day. Sure. But I was going to make my day. I guess the kid in me took over and I grinned. Larry "Buck" Owen turned back to look at me. I mouthed "Thank you," and he tipped his cap. My life complete, I waited until I got back to my seat to examine my prize, which was the most beautiful baseball I had ever seen, with its grass stain, infield dirt, and smudge of pine tar. I held it up, like a precious orb. My dad smiled but said nothing.

Prizes were given out during the game, as part of Fan Appreciation Night. My Atlanta Braves lost, but I won a fully cooked 20-lb. ham.

Buck

The Braves finished the season with 66 wins and 96 losses, fifth place in the National League West.

I sent Larry Owen a note of thanks, but I could never express what that simple act meant to me. He passed away in 2018. His obituary stated that among his many accomplishments he was also a catcher for the Atlanta Braves.

Thirty-eight years later now, I still have that ball and no regrets about keeping it for myself. Like I said, baseball brings out the kid in me.

Thanks, Buck. *Play ball!* •

Copyright 2024, M.J. Norwood

Constant writer and occasional author M. J. Norwood lives in East Bend, North Carolina. Her work has appeared in previous Personal Stores Project publications *Curious Stuff* and *Twists and Turns*.
A member of the North Carolina Writers' Network, and active in Yadkin County's Between the Covers Book Club, she is currently writing her third novel, and avidly supporting the Atlanta Braves.

Searching for Archibald
by Phyllis Castelli

Lallie Smith was two months shy of her sixth birthday when her mother was buried on a cold, clear Tuesday in March 1906. I imagine a sad, confused little girl in the arched doorway of Plank Chapel Methodist Church, taking her father's hand before crossing the dirt road to the cemetery.

On a cold, clear Tuesday in February 1915, Lallie's father, Archibald, was laid to rest beside her mother, right where I found them both 75 years later.

In the early 1990s, genealogy was still mostly fieldwork: following a grandparent's foggy recollections, copying names from crumbling family bibles, and deciphering courthouse records. Churchyard burial plots were first-rate storytellers. Back then, my Uncle Durwood and I often roamed the countryside in his old red pickup truck, hunting for graves.

Those old roads were my uncle's childhood stomping grounds, rich with memories of tobacco barns and swimming holes. When I could not find my elusive great-grandfather, Durwood became my guide. We explored many peaceful old graveyards, rubbing our hands over worn sandstone markers to feel words no longer seen. Sadly, the search for Archibald Smith seemed futile.

Uncle Durwood married Daddy's sister, Earlene, the year I turned 1. Before each adventure, my aunt insisted we visit around their kitchen table. "First things first," she would say, taking Blue Willow mugs from the cabinet. Usually, Earlene was only vaguely interested in ancestry, absently listening while pouring coffee. One day, out of the blue, she asked if I had found Archibald. I shook my head, "No. I'm about ready to give up."

Earlene looked at Durwood, "I remember Daddy talking about cousins at Old Plank Chapel." She raised her eyebrows, "You know it's just down the road."

Durwood smiled sheepishly, "Should have gone there first."

I strained to glimpse the church as Uncle Durwood drove, but trees and the slightly curved road obscured the view. When the truck slowed, I saw a gleaming white clapboard church on a grassy rise: Plank Chapel. A trio of stained-glass windows adorned the front wall, and a shining cross atop a steeple pointed through the clear blue sky to heaven.

The red truck's tires crunched on the cemetery's graveled through-road. From the window, I saw two white sandstone monuments engraved "Smith." The next few moments seemed to pass by in slow motion. Walking carefully to the first stone in the plot, we looked down and read "Archibald A. Smith, 1847-1915." Uncle Durwood placed his hand on my shoulder,

"Well, there he is." My great-grandmother rested beside her husband. Great uncles, aunts, and cousins lay nearby. There was an immediate sense of joyful connection. The years between us evaporated like mist in sun. It felt like a family reunion where, at any moment, someone would offer sweet, iced tea and pecan pie.

Archibald was born into 60 years of history in the Plank Chapel congregation. His grandfather was a trustee for the first church building in 1790. Arch's father, a revered pastor, was known for hellfire and brimstone sermons at days-long camp meetings. Looking over my shoulder at that religious fervor, I am surprised my modern-day family was not more devout.

In 1927, my grandfather, Lallie's big brother, moved from the farm into town and joined First Methodist Church. Their children and grandchildren were members but off-and-on churchgoers, except for me. I was at the church almost daily for piano lessons, choir practice, handbell rehearsals, and Sunday services. The music seeped into my bones.

A framed photo of a Christmas Eve worship service hangs near my piano. In it, my choir and I are standing in a chancel loft, wearing red robes with white stoles. Watchful, the organist awaits my cue. I remember lifting my hands to conduct the anthem. The sweetness of the music ebbed and flowed between us until the hushed amen.

We are imprinted by many things in this life, as surely as a painter's brushstrokes leave intentional images on a canvas. We are the patchwork quilt of granddaddy's stories, rocking chairs on a wide porch, and the butterbeans and fried chicken of family dinners. We carry a light heart from one grandmother and a tinge of melancholy from another. I began my church music career unaware of my Plank Chapel story. Now, I feel the thread of DNA knitting generations of Smiths together with far more than dark hair.

Some years ago, Earlene and Durwood hosted a family picnic. Most of my parents' generation were no longer among the living. I turned to my cousin, Debby, and asked, "Where are all the old people?"

She looked at me with a wry smile. "Honey, it's us."

Things are different now. In his mid-90s, Uncle Durwood is housebound. Aunt Earlene is gone. Debby is gone.

Lallie died in 1982.

Old Plank Chapel remains my family touchstone, and I know exactly where to find Archibald. •

Copyright 2024, Phyllis Castelli

Phyllis Castelli returned home to Henderson, North Carolina, after retirement from her music career. She spends time with her lifetime special interests: writing, music, photography, a pollinator garden, and Black Labrador Retrievers. Phyllis loves to create projects that knit together the beauty of those favorites. Phyllis's poems and essays have appeared in *Quillkeepers Press*, *The Avocet*, *Scarlet Leaf Review*, and *Tar River Poets*, among others. As a young poet, she published *Gentle, I Think*, a book of poems with pen and ink illustrations.

Wild Things
by Mick Scott

I first learned about the Russian domesticated foxes of San Diego in April 2020.

At that point I'd been studying foxes—colorful, fleet creatures —for a couple of years, obsessively, reading textbooks as well as folktales; watching PBS documentaries followed by Disney cartoons. I'd been learning about their families, usually comprised of a daddy fox, a mommy fox, and a new litter of three to seven kits every spring; their characteristics: cautious, but playful and energetic; their range and diet: living pretty much everywhere except New Zealand and Antarctica, and eating voles, mice, squirrels, fruits, and veggies; and the way they've adjusted to us. They're canny enough to live in urban settings while avoiding too much contact with these big, furless things who sometimes react to them with unthinking fear and the threat of violence.

I also began to observe them, one leash in particular (one term for a family group) that lives in a field near my home, getting close enough, regularly enough, that they became accustomed to my presence. I watched them play and raise their young. I recognized them as individuals and gave them names: Sally

Forth, Scruffy Milton, Scalawag. I wrote about these foxes regularly in the Winston-Salem Journal, where I was, until last year, the editorial page editor.

Many of us treasure these lovely neighbors, including a network of wildlife rehabbers and rescue organizations that heal their injuries and protect them from harm. Some have tried to turn them into pets, but such attempts usually end in heartache. They're too wild, as nature intended.

A group of Russian scientists had different ideas, though, back in 1959, when they began a breeding program with the hope of producing a friendlier, tamer canid. Sixty generations later, they succeeded, according to the Judith A. Bassett Canid Education and Conservation Center outside San Diego. The center's founders, David and Amy Bassett, brought three of them to the U.S. in 2016 and enlisted them as fox ambassadors. The foxes interact pleasantly with human visitors and seem to actually *like* them. Every indication is that they're healthy and happy.

When I learned about them, I immediately wanted to see them.

But this information arrived just as COVID was beginning to impose its limitations on us. San Diego took its place on my short list of unattainable dream destinations, including English Harbour, Newfoundland; Sark Island off the coast of France; Iceland's Ring Road; cold Ulaanbaatar; the Bruder Klaus Field Chapel in rural Germany.

A year later, we'd learned to live with the virus. And when
I saw that airline prices had fallen dramatically, it hit me:
If I don't go now, I might never go. There will always be
a reason to postpone the trip. I must go now, before I find
a rationale to stop myself.

I booked my flight. I spoke to the Bassetts and learned as
much as I could about the three Russians who had migrated
to California. Though the public can visit them in groups every
weekend, I booked a private session, one hour with just the
foxes, a facilitator, and me.

And finally, the hour came. Victor, a classic red fox with white
chest and black socks, hopped into my lap and begged me
to scratch his back; sweet Maksa (short for Maksamilian),
with snow-white fur (a melanin variation) and candy corn ears
(red melting into black), planted her front paws on my leg and,
I swear, smiled at me; and Mikhail, called a silver fox because
of his coloring (salt-and-pepper except for the bright white tip
of his brush), lapped chunks of chicken from my palm as
I stroked his fur, then gently nibbled my fingers.

It was magical.

But despite their ease with me, and my wonder at their gentle
nature, I felt no real bond with them. They weren't "my" foxes.
They were a novelty.

I returned home to the foxes I know, wild things that will
never be petted like their cousins.

Meeting the Russian foxes was an incredible trip into a liminal fantasy world. But they pay a price for their domestication: They could never survive on their own. They'll never choose their own companions. They'll never be angry or afraid.

The wild foxes' fierce, cunning spirit sends them to ramble at will, loving and fighting, speaking their own secret patois, with sightings as rare as those of ghosts or Bigfoot. They run silently through the woods, sleep on the open ground with their brushes wrapped over their paws, hunt exactingly in the rain. Their kits peek at me from behind foliage, from behind their mothers' flanks, until they decide for themselves that I'm no threat. Then we see each other as we are.

As nature intended. •

Copyright 2024, Mick Scott

Winston-Salem-native Mick Scott worked in the Winston-Salem Journal's editorial department for 20 years, the last five of those as editorial-page editor. During that time, he churned out thousands of editorials and opinion columns on tight deadline and received numerous first- and second-place awards from the N.C. Press Association. He is the author of *Stardust and Scar Tissue: Rambles, Ruminations, and the Search for an Authentic Culture of Life*, published in 2023 by Press53. Follow Mick's current writing at mickscott.substack.com

Horsehair in the Hummingbird Nest
by Janet K. Baxter

One bright afternoon in May, I had yelled to my husband, "Michael, get the camera!" as I looked into the birthing stall and found Missy lying on her side straining to deliver her second foal. Opening the sliding wood door, I stepped in and sank along the wall to sit and watch the birth of my first, and only, filly. Melody came quickly. First two hooves, then the nose with the tongue torqued to one side, then the head and shoulders, her beautiful chestnut body, and finally her hips and long back legs slid in a wet pile. She ever so slowly sat up with her head bobbing and then, after many tumbles, stood. I noticed the flaxen mane and tail that lit up the filly, coloring her like her father. I was so excited to have been able to watch this birth and to have the filly colored the way I had hoped. I even sent email birth announcements to my trail riding friends.

This was the second foal to be born at my barn. After my first foal's surprise birth at 2 a.m. during a torrential rainstorm, I had again arranged video feed to be sent to the television in our sunroom to monitor the mare during the night. Each night, I dutifully woke once or twice to check on Missy via the camera positioned high in the corner of her stall. With the first foal, I had overslept my usual check time and, looking anxiously at the grainy screen, found a tiny form staggering around the stall looking for mom to nurse. Noah was an hour or two old by that time. I had missed the birth.

I decided to keep Melody and train her as my primary trail riding horse. With her, I proudly had a chestnut with flaxen mane and tail, good temperament, and a smooth Tennessee Walking Horse ride. I was in my early 50's at that time. I often calculated how old I would be once she turned 10, or 15, or 20. Would I still be riding? I was planning on it, laughingly saying I was going to ride until I was 95.

As I slowly ambled toward my late 50's and with my 60's not too far around the bend, I was faced with life's reality (the body does age, *bummer!*) and a conundrum. Could I breed my black mare one more time and get the silver dapple foal I longed for? Should I?

Breeding for a silver dapple is a bit of a gamble. Pairing a silver dapple stallion with a black mare finds only a 50-50 chance of having a silver dapple foal. Pairing two silver horses together was not an option, as there was a high risk for eye problems with that genetic combination. I had a well-bred black mare, Jewel, that I had purchased just for this pairing years before, but should I breed for a foal at this stage of *my* life? I had bred Jewel once before, but the pregnancy did not take; and, as the economy went into a recession, I was grateful not to have responsibility for an extra horse. However, as "almost 60" sidled up on me, the thought of a silver dapple foal kept punctuating my thoughts. I could, yes; but should I? I would be 70 when that youngster turned 12, which is about the best age for a seasoned trail horse. Would I still be riding at that time?

Year after year, strong fall winds bring a cascade of autumn-colored leaves like heavy rain drops after a storm. In the same winds, hummingbird nests also tumble from the crepe myrtle trees that dot our acreage. These tiny momma birds choose the soft light-colored horsehair they find in the pasture to line the bottom of their nests each spring. When the grandchildren visit, I show each nest. "Look," I say enthusiastically pointing to the flaxen or silver horsehair lining the bottom of each little bowl, smaller than the cup of my hand. "There's Melody's light hair!" and "There's Nugget's silver hair!"

I did breed Jewel to a striking silver dapple stallion. Nugget joined my herd during spring 13 years ago. And, like that first foal, I also missed that birth. Even with a new camera in the barn, Jewel sneaked that birth beneath the camera range one very dark night, although I did see Nugget sitting up when he was just a few minutes old.

Before I ride now, I carefully wash Nugget. His silver mane and tail glitter in the breeze and his silver dapples prominently show below his new saddle. With each ride on this handsome boy, I am secretly delighted that I took that chance. My flaxen and silver memories make me smile. •

Copyright 2024, Janet K. Baxter

Janet K. Baxter lives in Kings Mountain, North Carolina, and is a member of the Charlotte Writer's Club and Scribblers, a memoir critique group. Her stories, "Horse Whispering for the Average Woman," "Southern Blues," "A Frank Lesson," "Cappie, The Boomerang Horse," "An Angel's Smile," "Morgan: Our Escape Artist," "One Soul Alone," and "Forest Bathing on Horseback" appeared in previous anthologies published by the Personal Story Publishing Project. Retired, Janet enjoys thread painting, trail riding, writing, and all the delights of her "mini-estate": www.mountaingaitacres.com.

Modes and Memories
by Edith Gettes

The Andante from Bach's 2nd unaccompanied violin sonata features a persistent pulse in one voice, while melody weaves around it in others, comforting, beautiful and haunting. I offered to perform it for the memorial service of my cherished friend, Sarah, her own voice silenced by ovarian cancer within months after retiring from the hospital where we worked together. Years had passed since I had played the piece, and as I attempted to resurrect the layered pitches and intricate bowings, a familiar sense of frustration and self-deprecation crept upon me, strengthening the loneliness of grief.

Hoping to transform the isolating self-critique into memory and motivation, I searched YouTube for a video recording. I was perusing resultant thumbnails when a familiar face startled me. There was no cigarette and his thick black hair had thinned gray, but Yuval was just as I remembered. Dimples made it appear he harbored a slight grin, while the violin balanced on his collar bone with bow held delicately between right thumb and middle finger. I felt a flurry of goosebumps as I clicked the image, held my breath, and waited.

Seconds later, his tone billowed from the speaker. A dormant internal spark ignited, transporting me back several decades to Indiana University, where I stood in front of him, violin hanging off my left shoulder, and bow dangling from my right hand. Tension stiffened my body, restricted my breath, and narrowed my vision.

Yuval, whom students called "the King," had garnered international awards and a cultish following. Barely 30 years old at the time, his playing was legendary and he wore torment like a red velvet cape. In the first weeks at IU, when we violinists recognized each other by our inflamed neck calluses, and exchanged pleasantries designed to elicit information about our connections and virtuosity, "Whose studio are you in?" was a constant refrain. When I answered "Yuval," eyes would widen with concern. Phrases such as "You'll learn a lot if you survive" or "I hope you're tougher than you look" dribbled from sympathetic lips.

Each week at lesson time, I'd knock on his door and be ushered into the studio. Yuval might be practicing, arranging his desk, or meditating upon the ever-present cigarette, whose ashes were allowed to dangle precariously above his violin. He'd often say nothing and wait for me to begin. While some of my neurons engaged in playing, others monitored my teacher, willing him to interrupt. Letting me reach the final cadence meant he deemed my rendition beyond repair and might wordlessly resume cleaning his desk, leaving me to slink away, tail between my legs. Another possibility was ending my lesson with a choice phrase such as the heavily accented

"I am too disappointed, please return next week" or "Edith, you are marinating in the juices of frustration."

The anguish of these moments, however, was a small sacrifice for those when he flicked the ashes off his cigarette, placed it between his lips, and took up his instrument. With violin cradled between left jaw and shoulder, he balanced his bow atop the strings, and spun a sonic web that danced around us. The strands of sound were varied and vital, constantly changing color, shape, and countenance. At once, he controlled and was enchanted by their capricious curves, which threatened to evade his grasp.

Bach's Chaconne, as performed by Yuval, emerged from the laptop's speakers. My grief seemed to liquify and flow through each meticulous phrase, muddling boundaries around composer, performer, and audience, between beauty and loss, past and present, even life and death.

Feeling motivated and nostalgic, I looked for more of his recordings. My search yielded more videos posted the same date, June of 2020, though most were recorded at other times. I imagined Yuval overcoming his own insecurities to grapple with the horrors of COVID, as well as complications of a concert career, by performing virtually. I felt inspired and brave. Perhaps I, too, could transform my grief into something creative and comforting.

As I continued practicing for Sarah's memorial, layers of self-critique gave way to the soothing powers of music. Memory of the notes awakened, my ear became more focused on delineating harmony from melody, my fingers and bow more cooperative. My grief and loneliness yielded to the pleasure and privilege of joining lives by music rather than by tragedy.

I cannot be certain of how my performance affected Sarah's mourning friends and relatives. I, however, was stronger, more grateful for music and more accepting of my imperfections. I think Sarah would have liked that. •

Copyright 2024, Edith Gettes

Edith Gettes has worked as a violinist, teacher, and psychiatrist, as well as mother of four daughters. She has lectured about learning, trauma, and motherhood at several international conferences. In addition to writing for musical and medical journals, her story "Banana Bread" appeared in the Personal Story Publishing Project's fall 2023 publication, *Sooner or Later*. Edith currently lives, works, plays, and writes in Asheville, North Carolina, where she is a member of the Flatiron Writers Room and NC Writers Network.

Getting High with Second Chances
by Ginny Grulke

Pearled drops of rain slowly slid down the bus window. In the late January afternoon, darkness had begun to drop over the city. Beyond the window, the Denver storefronts blurred as the lumbering bus quickened its slow pace from the bus station.

Anticipation and nervousness tightened my chest as I thought about the days to come. At 71 years old, was this a foolish decision? Or a brave one?

A sweet diesel smell filled the bus as the engine vibration pulsed my seat: subtle warnings of my last opportunity to change my mind.

Attending college in the 1960's and '70's, I had watched in amazement as students marched in the streets, protesting the Vietnam War.

I stared as young men ignited their draft cards, the flames blazing.

I held my breath as women torched their bras in an act of defiance.

From the safety of the dormitory, I saw throngs of students thrown into an 18-wheeler truck, headed for the county jail after a sit-in at the towering administration building.

Headlines roared "WOODSTOCK!" as thousands converged on a New England pasture for rock music, weed and unveiled sex on muddy blankets.

San Francisco birthed the "free love" movement, with barefoot hippies cohabiting in rundown houses, smoking dope and experimenting with psychedelic drugs.

Timothy Leary preached his revolutionary message: "turn on, tune in, drop out."

But I lacked the bravery to participate in the most momentous, historical period of my life. Frozen by my traditional upbringing, I obeyed the rules: Respect authority. Obey the law. Go to church. Work hard.

The camaraderie of fighting against "The Man" and being arrested for your values passed me by. I didn't show up for those who left unwillingly for the Killing Fields of Southeast Asia. I cheered from the sidelines for women who fought to throw off their second-class status.

I dutifully attended all of my classes and slumped over hours of homework each night. I was poor and needed a good job. Poverty was my alibi, although others just as poor were out on the battlefield, fighting for a voice.

The shameful truth was that I lacked the courage to challenge the status quo, even as I admired those who did.

For over fifty years, I carried the guilt of that brain-washed fear. I had to redeem myself, and it had to be soon. I couldn't recreate the atmosphere of those earlier days. But I joined Pro-Choice protests and resolved to try marijuana. Would a marijuana high assuage my regrets and teach me something about myself?

Weed; Now or Never.

I enrolled in a 2-day "Psychedelic Cannabis" session in Boulder, Colorado, where cannabis is legal. This hefty bus would deliver me, late to the party and long overdue, to my salvation.

As the miles rolled past, I stared out of the rain-smeared window. What if this was too much for me to handle? What if it was, in fact, psychedelic? Or, on the other extreme, what if the marijuana was not powerful, and I'd spent my time and money on a pipe dream?

The next day at the clinic, I got acclimated to smoking, inhaling marijuana until its effects hijacked my brain. Technicolor visions rapidly appeared out of the haze.

I was riding a horse down a forest trail, followed by a group of wild horses with a cartoon appearance: fat legs, flat hooves, wavy manes and big eyes. I felt unspeakable joy, leading the charge at a full gallop, unsure of where we were going or why. The wind blew in my hair, with the thudding sound of my herd behind me, following me unafraid.

In the next vision, different animals trailed me down a woodland path. All of my friends were there: Bambi,

Thumper, Peppy LePew, and George of the Jungle. All had large Disneyesque eyes and happy-go-lucky smiles. The sun filtered through the trees, the leaves were unnaturally bright green, and the path was soft and wide. I charged ahead, again full of joy, with no idea where we were going. They trusted me to take them there.

This vision morphed into the bittersweet. My dead husband lay on a litter, covered with a shroud, carried by four tall Africans. They entered a small cave, lowered him gently, and left quietly. I walked into the cave, pulling back the shroud and touching him to make sure he was truly dead. He was. Turning around and walking away, I didn't look back or cry. I disappeared into the forest.

On the bus back to Denver, my mind was filled with these enchanting visions. I reflected on their meanings. I wanted more: more marijuana, more insight. At last, I had captured the bravery I lacked so many years ago.

It was a start. •

Copyright 2024, Ginny Grulke

Ginny Grulke lives in Lexington, Kentucky, where she has discovered a community of like-minded writers through the Carnegie Center for Literacy and Learning. She has been writing non-fiction for her family and friends to enjoy. Her stories revolve around a life with horses, aging, and widowhood, as well as her rural childhood in a large Pennsylvania Dutch family. A few colorful relatives and horses have been inspirations for her stories. She enjoys taking common place situations and looking deeper to find an understanding of people and the animals they keep.

Green-eyed Lady, Not My Type
by Bob Amason

Mrs. June Brown had green eyes. Well, green contacts, anyway. In 1966 she was the high priestess of the typewriter at Glynn County Junior High. Her incantations were rhythmic and hypnotic: "A, S, D, F, J, K, L, Semi." It would have been perfect if she had thrown in "eye of newt." The class, consisting mostly of girls, slammed a key with every word.

I was only taking typing because I needed an elective, and some nitwit told me that typing was easy. Liar. Thank God it was only half a year.

The keys were capped to obscure the letters and encourage 'touch typing.' Hell, I thought it was all touch typing. Didn't you touch the keyboard? Perhaps this attitude led me to making a sparkling D in 8th-grade typing.

Mrs. Brown looked at me hard with her green contacts and said, "If you don't care, I don't care." She was the "pompatus" of the typewriter, and I was pretty sure she was in league with some kind of demon to ruin my life. It wasn't that I didn't care, I just wasn't enthusiastic.

Green-eyed Lady, Not My Type

I scraped by with that D because I hit some absolute minimum number of correct characters in some idiotic phrase about quick brown foxes. No amount of practice would improve my typing. Didn't need to know how to touch type, anyway.
I would be some kind of engineer or executive and never need to type again. It was 1966, remember.

In a supreme irony, I am a professional writer some three score years later. I type not to make writing easier but as an integral aspect of the art of forming ideas on paper. It's been a long journey.

In 1982, I went to a computer store in Sacramento, California, and inquired about buying a computer. I was an Air Force officer, but I thought it might be cool to be a novelist.
I thought I might whip out some interesting stories about flying B-52s.

I thought a computer might make it easy and help me avoid the dozens of mistakes in my typing. I knew I'd make the same number of errors, but at least I would avoid spending a fortune on that liquid correction fluid. And if you remember that, you probably also remember carbon paper; but I digress.

I couldn't see spending $3500 on a computer and software, so I postponed becoming a novelist for ... about 45 years. Besides, my squadron mate, Dale Brown, beat me to writing exciting stories about flying B-52s.

I escaped further typing until Mat, my new boss at a unit of the Air Staff, said, "I need you to get on the computer and email our subordinate units. Ask them to … blah, blah, blah." In no time, I was seated before a glowing green screen. A monster with one green eye. You'd think Mrs. Brown was looking at me.

At that moment—I confess before God—I knew nothing about computers. Nada. Nunca. Zip. Zero. The little Charlie Chaplin character in the computer ads said it was easy to use a computer. Liar.

Worse, I was still a miserable typist. Mrs. Brown proved that in 1966.

Mat didn't let up. "Here's a list of shortcuts…you just type CTRL+KQ to quit." I immediately asked if that meant I could quit the organization with the push of a button. He laughed; I was serious. Despite hitting CTRL+KQ about a thousand times, I was still stuck in that unit, so I spent the next three years learning to use computers…and typing. A lot.

Mat, one of my closest friends these 40 years, helped inspire me to become a writer. I didn't know it then, but he did. He assigned me to lead a 30-person team reviewing U.S. Air Force war plans. While everyone on the team had input, I wrote the final 200-page report. On a computer. Thanks, Mat, I think.

In a succession of military assignments, I must have typed five million words, maybe more. I got better at typing in self-defense. You'd think I'd have learned a lesson, but I retired from the USAF and became a college professor: nothing but typing. Teaching online, I typed every day for 25 years.

Green-eyed Lady, Not My Type

To prove the wisdom of being careful what you wish for, I retired from teaching and became a novelist. More typing. I recently published my seventh novel. It's about flying. Hope it's as good as Dale Brown's work. I should have done it sooner.

Maybe priestesses of the keyboard are immortal changelings. Mrs. Brown, wherever you are and however you keep showing up in my life, *thank you*. I still feel your green eyes on me. I do care, after all.

I should have said that a long time ago.

CTRL+KQ.
Roger that. •

Copyright 2024, Bob Amason

Award-winning author Bob Amason is a retired US Air Force Lieutenant Colonel and college professor. A Florida Writer's Association member, Bob writes under his pen name, Frank A. Mason. His Journeyman Chronicles series of American Revolutionary War novels are Amazon.com bestsellers. *Journeyman: Heart of Tempered Steel* won the 2023 Florida Writer's Association Gold Royal Palm Literary Award, Florida's most prestigious writing prize. Bob's writing has been published in four anthologies, academic journals, and books. He lives in Florida with his overachieving wife, a professor who is the author of a series of children's books.

The News
by Barbara Reese Yager

The nurse says my gynecologist will talk to me on Monday.

"No, absolutely not," I spit back. "I am not waiting and wondering if I have cancer until Monday." I say it softly but with full vigor. It is a summer Friday afternoon at the bank. Many in the Marketing Department have left for the day; a few die-hards are still working in their cubes.

"The doctor is with a patient, and I don't know how long he will be," the nurse echoes.

"That's fine. I don't care how long I have to hold on. I want him to speak to me today," I whisper as fiercely as I can.

"Ok. I'll tell him," the nurse agrees.

It is a long wait. I don't know if there is hold music or not. It doesn't matter. My head is swimming. My heart is pumping hard. I am barely keeping it together. Outside, sunshine lights the Carolina blue sky.

Finally, Dr. Willis comes on and says "Mrs. Yager?" Oh, that's my so newly minted "Mrs.," I think.

"Yes," I acknowledge.

"I am so sorry to say the biopsy came back positive." He waits a beat. I hear him sigh, and then go on, "Do you have a preference for a surgeon or oncologist?"

"Ah, no," I murmur in my tiny voice.

"Okay. We will make those appointments for you on Monday. My office will call you with that information." He says, "Again, I am so sorry."

"Yes, thank you very much for telling me," I respond in my best Miss Manners way.

What is my first step? I call my best friend at work and ask, "Can you drive me home?" Yes, of course. She walks over to my cubicle with her purse and laptop case. She knows by my face not to ask why. Silently, we go down in the office elevator and into the cool, dark, parking garage.

When we sit in her car I say, "I have breast cancer."

"Mmmm. How can I help?" is her first question. She is always this marvelous.

"I don't know. I have to tell Don first."

I exhale.

On that day in August, we had been married for six months. Six amazing months of bursting love. Our Valentine's Day wedding was a spectacular, Renaissance-themed party with our children, our families, and our friends. We were blissfully happy. We were hopeful about our future.

Would there be one?

No conversation is required in the car. Linda reaches over to squeeze my arm and leaves her hand there. I know cancer is a death sentence, but nothing else. What do I know? I married a good man, one who lives by the adage, "I have your back." When I'm in the proverbial ditch, he digs feverishly with the biggest shovel until I stand on firm ground. When I'm upset and talk and talk and talk, my husband waits for the silence then leans over to hold my hand. He is all in.

At our house, my friend offers to come in, but I demur. I can't string two words together. I am bursting to cry. She hugs me hard and I go in. The dogs greet me as if I have been gone all day. I have, of course. They don't care about my news. Mommy is home. I bend down to hug Bentley, my best boy dog, until he wiggles away. I go to the microwave to make myself a hot tea with lemon. Even in summertime, it's my comfort drink.

I stand at the kitchen window waiting for my husband to walk through the door. I think of this moment as when my newly married life begins. When I belong to him. Safe in his arms.

The News

The lemon in the hot tea wafts beneath my nose. Bentley leans heavily against my leg. I'm weighed down by the doctor's news. No, no, now my news. How do I say there's no happily ever after?

The sleigh bells on the back door alert the dogs and they rush to smother Don. I hear him say "Were you good puppies today? Did no one run away?" The air conditioner starts, and I feel the cold air glide over the kitchen floor around our feet. I look up with tears streaming.

"What's wrong? What's wrong?" he fervently whispers.

I swallow hard, but the news offers no joy. •

Copyright 2024, Barbara Reese Yager

Barbara Reese Yager is a writer who draws inspiration from life on her farm with dogs and horses and her love for her family and friends. She was a winner of the Charlotte Writers Ruth Moose Fiction contest. Barbara's work appeared in an anthology of non-fiction, Sooner or Later by the Personal Story Publishing Project, Daniel Boone Footsteps Publisher. She holds a BS in Human Development from Penn State and a MS in Leadership from Duquesne University. She is a member of the Charlotte Writers Club and Charlotte Lit. Tales of her life can be found at waggintailfarm.com.

Where Angels Fear
by Cherie Cox

"**C**ome with me to Italy, Buddy," she implored my father. "Let's travel."

In her 40th year, Mother had become "a decided redhead," brightening her interests in a broader world. Married at World War II's end, she had reared five children and supported his ministry.

Father nicknamed her "Lucy," with good cause, although her name was Marie. Her fiery independence was not always appreciated by anyone expecting meekness.

"I thought I was marrying a shy, soft-spoken beauty," he once said.

The ministry had taken a toll on her and on him by their 20th anniversary. A divisive church in Baltimore, Maryland, had tested their foundations, maritally and spiritually. Mid-winter, they moved back to North Carolina. A fire in their tinder-box rental house destroyed almost all their worldly goods.

They moved again to another town, another rental. He took a job on a newspaper and pastored appreciative rural churches which lacked the budget for a fulltime minister. Their fifth child was born in 1964, a change-of-life surprise.

"I'll mind the kids," he said. "You take the trip. I've seen all the world I need to see."

During the War years, he joined the Navy and left college. He served in the South Pacific theater, including ports of call like Hong Kong, Singapore, the Philippines and, eventually, Tokyo.

She had also left college and served as a clerk typist in Washington, D.C., for two years. They had never dated.

She wrote many pen pals throughout the world, including him and one Italian, who wanted her to learn the language. Both wanted a photograph of the dark-eyed, petite woman. Father posted his, inscribed "the girl I hope to marry."

"If that's what you get for going to church, Buddy, I'm going to start," one sailor said. Onboard the carrier escort, shipmates called Father "the little preacher." His affable nickname stuck. Admiration for his informal worship services, good character and approachability endured. He also manned a .50 caliber machine gun when the ship was attacked.

"I never thought I would marry a minister," Mother once confided. But she envisioned him as a natural father.

When the blue-eyed veteran returned from war, he brought her a teakwood chest containing a bronze silk robe. Then he proposed marriage. Mother wore the robe to celebrate each child's birth.

When she traveled without him to Florence, Italy, she would

express her independence. A native Italian offered to show her "the City tourists never see." We never quite knew what that meant. But Michelangelo's 17-foot-tall statue of David "took my breath away," she said. The Golden Doors, called the Gates of Paradise by Ghiberti, also figured in her epic stories.

She returned to us with a three-foot marble statue of a child and a visionary's mist in her eyes. But her suitcase and her camera had been stolen at an American airport. Father drove through several states to bring her safely home. He might have been exhausted. But she was exuberant.

"I could have died happily in Florence."

"You almost did, Marie."

He admitted missing her terribly after the luxury of a few days in a quiet house with their moping 4-year-old boy. Their relationship blossomed again.

She had traveled where angels dwell in Italy. She had also traveled where angels fear to tread in ministry. Between moving so often through Texas, Maryland, and back through the Carolinas, and never owning a home, her sacrifices had once circumscribed her dreams. When he sacrificed for her to fly to Italy, she re-energized.

Mother cherished her familial role more in those unexpectedly few years following her world travels. Although she never finished college, together, they assured all five children did. In 1984, Father fell asleep at 60 years of age and entered those Gates of Paradise, much too early for our acceptance.

The last rental home belonged to the newspaper employer and that required her to make another move. Father had hoped to retire from newspaper work and had just returned to fulltime ministry, called by a dedicated church who valued his interim pastoral work.

"You done good, Buddy," his brother-in-law, a lay minister, eulogized.

Mother assuaged her sorrow with comforting words, often repeated through her 98 years: "His feet never touched the ground."

Truthfully, they were both visionaries. Born in the 1920s, they grew up with dreams during the Depression. They survived a world war with faith intact. Their lives resided with a higher power and with their children's wellbeing. They trusted each other enough to build a marriage and a family in a fragile world. That is still a scary proposition today. As a Baby Boomer child, I am glad they took the chance and took the trip. •

Copyright 2024, Cherie Cox

A published news journalist and a practiced lawyer, Cherie Cox calls North Carolina home. Awards include the Charlotte Writers' Club first place in poetry. Published short stories, essays, professional legal articles and poetry vary her credentials. These include Personal Story Publishing Project anthologies, *Kakalak,* and *The Christmas Wreath.* She enjoys people who give their best effort. *The Hickory Daily Record* and the Mecklenburg County Public Defender's Office enriched her life. Many individuals inspire her respect for the written word.

Then and Now
by Patricia Joslin

It's time. My boxes are packed, or most of them anyway. I've lived in this apartment for nearly five years. It's been a comfortable place to find my way in the world as an independent woman. My neighbors are generally kind, but nameless. Most of them are professionals in their 30's who work in the city. I joke that I am the "oldest living person" in the complex!

Closets and cabinets have been sorted to downsize my possessions. Last year I sold the king size bed and replaced it with a queen. In July, my dining table went to a friend, as did the storage shelves in the locker I no longer needed. Habitat Restore recently collected two worn loveseats and an overstuffed chair. All my photos have been digitized and now have a home on Google Photos. It's actually been fun scanning and reliving the past.

I'm looking forward to moving into the new building that opens in a few weeks. It's just two blocks from where I live now. My apartment will be on the ninth floor overlooking the canopy of neighborhood trees and the steeple of my church. The decision to move was not easy, but my adult children are relieved that this move is happening now while I am in relatively good health. The senior community is designed to be a safe and inviting place for me to grow into the next chapter of my life. I imagine it will be like living on a luxury cruise ship with lots of interesting people and activities, a great fitness facility, and wonderful food. I hope so.

Today a friend called to chat while the wind blew strong, and rain pelted my windows. Though the day was gloomy, she shared that she has decided that now is the time to move past her depression to fill her days with wonder and delight. Book clubs, church discussions, dinner with friends is how she is choosing to live. We agreed that when we focus on the positives, all is well, and we get a good night's sleep. Some would say I am a cup-half-full person, or maybe even a full-cup person. I'm feeling upbeat about the transitions ahead, yet I know that I'll need to be flexible and ready to pivot at times.

So much of life is out of our control. About the only real control I have is managing my breath when in yoga. During our early retirement years, my husband and I traveled to Europe, and even chose to live in Italy for a month. He learned to speak Italian. I leaned on his communication skills and smiled a lot, which always works well with shopkeepers and vintners. But then my husband was diagnosed with pancreatic cancer. Those days of unknowing, days of pain and suffering became days to breathe into each moment. Perhaps that's how all of us should live our lives, paying attention to each moment, consciously breathing. I sometimes forget to do that, but I try.

I also try to stay healthy, eat right, and exercise. But when COVID arrived the whole world felt out of control. In the early days of the emerging pandemic, I happened to be on a trip to South America as a solo traveler, only to be told that I needed to return to the U.S. while I could still get a flight home. Since then, we've learned to manage the virus by vaccinating and taking precautions. Now we live with a better understanding of our risks. But good health is not guaranteed. A few months after COVID entered the picture, I was diagnosed with Type 1 Diabetes. I now control my blood sugar with my diet and insulin.

When I sold my home a few years ago, I left behind beautiful gardens. I had been a Master Gardener, knew what I grew, volunteered to keep public gardens weed-free. I no longer garden, so I created a new outlet. I am a writer. What first began as "literary therapy" following my husband's death is now an activity that brings me great joy, and new friends. I take classes, spend time thinking and writing, and meet with an online poetry group each month. My first poetry chapbook was published last year, and I've built a website. As Ralph Waldo Emerson said, "Every artist was first an amateur." I am first and still an amateur.

When my boxes are unpacked in that ninth-floor apartment next month, I am sure to find things that I no longer need, perhaps that old soup pot or the well-used wok. I've learned that life is like that in other ways, too. Sometimes we need to give up relationships or places or things that no longer add positives to our lives. I know that within each chapter of this

Then and Now

book called life, things change. Sometimes dramatically. Change keeps me humble and excited about the pages, the chapters, to come. •

Copyright 2024, Patricia Joslin

Patricia Joslin is a poet and essayist living in Charlotte, North Carolina. Her chapbook, *I'll Buy Flowers Again Tomorrow: Poems of Loss and Healing*, was published in 2023 by Charlotte Lit Press. Poems have appeared in *Kakalak*, *Tipton Poetry Journal*, *New Note Poetry*, *Eunoia Review*, and the *San Antonio Review*. Her essays have appeared in Personal Story Project anthologies in 2020, 2021 and 2023. She loves live jazz, chamber music, solo travel and full-bodied red wine. https://www.patriciajoslin.com/

Precious Treasure
by Martha Rowe Vaughn

A question posed by my mother started me on an adventure and took me into a mystery.

"Martha, do you want the old trunk that belonged to your grandmother Sallie? It's full of letters between her and your grandfather Dr. Rowe."

The trunk also contained the writings of several members of Dr. Rowe's family. One in particular caught my attention. In looping pencil script, Great Aunt Eugenia, Dr. Rowe's sister, wrote down the birth and death dates of all the family from 1808 to 1920s. She wrote, "Found in J. C.'s Bible at Lilly's house in the shelves to the right of the fireplace." Lilly was her older sister.

Joseph Columbus Rowe, Dr. Henry Rowe's father was a Methodist minister. J. C. as he was known then, reared six children by himself while ministering at numerous churches throughout western North Carolina. All their birth dates were listed in the Bible according to Eugenia. Was it possible that the Bible still existed? I knew where Lilly's house was, now

owned by her son-in-law's cousin. Might I find Joseph
Columbus's Bible? I decided to try.

J. C. was a man before his time and controversial because he
ministered to anyone, regardless of color or circumstances.
Through his letters, I had read his fatherly advice to his son
who was stationed at Edgewood Arsenal during World War I.
The letters were full of love, encouragement, and pride at his
son's accomplishments.

After reading my grandparents' letters, I decided to write
a book about them and to include my remembrances
of Grandma Sallie and my time with her. She showed me
that a woman can ride horses, shoot a gun, kill snakes, run
a business, sell real estate, tame an Arkansas wilderness, and
cook. I entitled the book *Grandma's Trunk*. I was still working
on it when I decided to find Great Grandfather's Bible.

I left for western North Carolina on the Bible quest. Arriving
at Lilly's house, I showed the current owner the writings from
Eugenia and explained who I was and what I was seeking. She
allowed me to come in and explore the shelves in the entry
room. She explained that the house was exactly like Lilly had
left it. She pointed out J. C.'s desk and Eugenia's oil paintings.

The owner left me to begin my search. Following Eugenia's
instructions, I found the Bible an hour later exactly where she
said it would be. My heart raced as I gently removed it and
held it in my hands. It was a small Bible covered in reddish-tan
leather, its spine missing, and the covers held on with heavy
thread. It felt warm to my touch. On the fly leaf written in my

Great Grandfather's script was the inscription: *Holy Bible, Book Devine, Precious Treasure, Thou art Mine. Joseph Columbus Rowe 1879*. Opening the Bible to the section between the Old and New Testament, I saw the marriage, death, and birth dates of the family, exactly as Eugenia had recorded them. Holding the Bible felt like a warm hand had crossed the years to hold my hand. I thought about J. C. and all he had been through ministering to hundreds of people in various churches, carrying his *Precious Treasure*. I did not want to let go. I wanted to possess the Bible. I could slip it into my briefcase and have it NOW. The owner would never know. *Steal my Great Grandfather's Bible?* What would he say? "Thou shalt not…" I couldn't do it. J. C. would not approve.

The owner came back into the room and snatched the Bible from my hand. I asked if I could have it. I offered to buy it. No was the firm and repeated answer. I put it back on the shelf. Never was the real answer. I left disappointed and broken-hearted.

Years went by. *Grandma's Trunk* was published and included the story about searching for the Bible. One day I went to the mailbox and there was a package wrapped in newsprint and tied with a red ribbon. It wasn't mailed, it was placed in the box by some unknown person. I opened it and was surprised to find J. C.'s Bible and a note written in a shaky hand:

Dear Martha,

As my most deserving direct descendent it is my wish and will that my Bible now be yours.

Precious Treasure

May God bless you—Lovingly,
J C Rowe

Never had turned into *forever*.

Years went by before the mystery was solved. A childhood friend read my book, *Grandma's Trunk*. He walked into Lilly's house, went to the shelf, found the Bible and walked out of the house with it and placed it in my mailbox. The owner never knew he was there. Bless him.

Precious Treasure, Thou art Mine. •

Copyright 2024, Martha Rowe Vaughn

Martha Rowe Vaughn lives in Mount Airy, North Carolina and is a member of a local writers group that has been meeting for over 15 years. During that time, she has published two books: *Grandma's Trunk* (non-fiction) and *Crossroads* (fiction). An interest in genealogy and family history prompted her to write both books. She graduated from the University of Kentucky with a degree in horticulture and owned and operated a tree nursery for 22 years. In retirement, she volunteers her horticulture knowledge and skill to local non-profit organizations.

A Drumbeat of Harp Strings
by Annie McLeod Jenkins

The refrain "it's now or never" pulsed in my youthful brain. *Do it now. Change now. Don't wait. Act now because your time is short.* I wonder if this drumbeat in my consciousness might be related to the required memorization of Longfellow's poem "A Psalm of Life" which exhorts "let us, then, be up and doing, with a heart for any fate." No matter the reason, my life has been richer and more nuanced because of the throb in my brain.

I was a student at Salem College in the late 1960s, an English major with a history minor, thinking of a Masters in English, perhaps leading to a teaching job. I was a typical young woman for this era, knowing that I wanted to work, but uncertain about what that meant. However, I did think that these years of college were a "last hurrah" for freedom to choose, experiment, expand, break the mold.

Music was something I loved but which was not my forte. I sang a bit, in the church choir and in a folk duet with a friend. I played the clarinet in the high school band. I could read music, but not well. I took piano lessons at age 12, but that lasted just six weeks because my teacher moved out of town.

Crazily, in my junior year at Salem, I decided to study harp. At that time at Salem, if you were a fulltime student who enrolled in private music lessons for credit, the cost was covered by tuition. The lessons seemed free. The harp professor, Patricia Pence (later Pence-Sokoloff), was the principal harpist with the Winston-Salem Symphony, and she had studied with Carlos Salzedo, the premier harpist in recent history. Why not jump in the deep end, right?

Looking back, I can see how nonsensical this decision was. I had never mastered a keyboard instrument, which would have made the path smoother, even if not completely crevice-free. I had no specific plan attached to this decision. Certainly, I did not expect to become a professional harpist, nor could I even afford to own an instrument. And yet, this decision enriched my life; it expanded my relationships, amplified my identity, helped me feel in control of my life path, and served as a perfect example of how plunging into uncharted territory can exhilarate.

My study of harp brought me into the sphere of so many colorful and talented people. First was my instructor, Pat Pence. One of the unexpected gifts from my fanciful foray into harp lessons was Pat's intuitive attention to the "me" who was the girl behind the harp strings. I am sure that my lessons were painful for her, with my stiff posture, my awkward hands, and my poor musicianship. Yet, she always greeted me with glee and warmth, as if I were her favorite pupil. Pat was, and is, "fey"; she could read my moods and drifting attention as if everything were written on my forehead. She was and continues to be a source of wonder in my life.

In addition to the rich relationship I formed with Pat, which is powerful even after 50 years, I also discovered a completely different academic family and way of thinking. Even the geography of my study was set apart. The Fine Arts Center was a place of seclusion. A harpist does not study in cooperation with other students. Harpists had no study groups; the requirement for improvement was time alone with the instrument. My new family included the Dean of the School of Music, who had to "hear" my exam for me to receive class credits. I also got to know numerous other creatives who populated the building: organists, pianists, vocalists, flutists—all inhabiting a place which I would never have known so intimately had I not scratched this itch. Just walking into the "catacombs," as we called the practice rooms, put me in a different universe. In fact, I wonder whether my brain waves might have been changed when I entered that space.

To this day, I am proud of the person who thought to herself, *do it now*. When I think about the kind of naïve bravery I summoned to dare this experience, I still can feel a boost to my ego. I have not touched a harp in years, but I continue to value how this decision to act raised my opinion of myself and gave me courage to try new things with less fear of failure. *Now or never* might seem a harsh directive, but for me, the result was increased joy, confidence, grit, and treasured personal relationships. •

Copyright 2024, Annie McLeod Jenkins

Annie McLeod Jenkins grew up in South Carolina around folks who were storytellers, so she became one too. Because she realized that no one else was going to tell her story, and with the opportunity that came with a slower life and a quieter house, she began writing down these personal recollections. She lives in Winston-Salem, NC, where she is a paying, but relatively inactive, member of Winston-Salem Writers. A few of her stories have appeared in earlier editions of the Personal Story Publishing Project.

Lifeguard
by Susan W. Harris

I felt his hand on the top of my head as he pushed me underwater. I squirmed and twisted my body to pop to the surface. After a gulp of air, I saw Benny grin as he grabbed me and pushed me down again. Out of breath and swallowing water, I remembered what my older brother told me if ever attacked, "Knee him in the balls!" So, I did.

This happened when I was 17. It was my third year as a camp counselor at Stonycroft Summer Camp about a mile from Lake Michigan in Shelby, Michigan. Close to passing my Red Cross Senior Lifesaving test with five other fellow counselors, we braced ourselves for the final step—an actual rescue. Liz, in her 30s and a University of Wisconsin swimming coach, served as the no nonsense waterfront director who administered the course. We swam miles of various strokes, learned the proper rescue holds, and took a written exam to reach this last step. We all drew names of a volunteer victim to rescue. That's when I drew "Benny," and my heart sank.

Benny Smith played fullback on his high school football team. He had over a hundred pounds on me and was a bully. He wouldn't dare bully campers, but I saw how he bullied other counselors and hired help. He asked me to go to movie night with him and also to a camp dance. I declined both. Benny hated rejection and held a grudge. I heard he was bad mouthing me.

When I kneed him, Benny screamed in pain, while the others on the dock bent over laughing. I did a straight-arm rescue, pulling him by his hair. Afterward, Liz told me, "I almost jumped in to help you, but you handled it." Liz did pass me for senior lifesaving, though my method of rescue was, she said, "unorthodox."

Having passed, I worked on the waterfront staff at Lake Stoney downhill from the camp. I proudly sewed my Senior Lifeguard badge to my 1957 modest, red, one-piece, swimsuit. Lifeguard duty was not easy. We swam laps before breakfast, no matter what the weather. Camper swimming periods were in the morning and afternoon. The waterfront area consisted of a T-shaped swimming dock, a small floating dock about 30 yards away and two areas for canoes and sailboats. Three lifeguards stood on the T-dock, one stationed on the floating dock and one manned the rowboat. Floating lines designated boundaries for the deep water that dropped off a ledge. We rotated positions every 30 minutes.

During that summer I began one afternoon shift on the floating dock with my whistle hanging around my neck, feeling a bit superior as a lifeguard. I felt the sun on my shoulders and smelled the familiar pine aroma. The squeals and laughter of the campers filled the air. Some of the campers played catch with a beach ball, including Bill, a 10-year-old boy. He had just passed his beginner swim test that qualified him to swim in the four-foot water. He was not a strong swimmer, but that's why I and the other lifeguards were there.

In their game of catch, the ball flew over the line, and Bill went after it, going past the ledge he didn't know about and into deep water. In an instant, he turned around with a frightened expression yelling, "Help!" He could no longer touch the bottom and he panicked. He went under. The boy bobbed up and struggled as he went down again. I looked around. Rod, in the rowboat, was too far. The guards on the dock were too far. I hesitated. I had never done a real rescue. For all my feelings of self-importance, I doubted my ability. I remembered how scared I felt when Benny pushed me under … my gulps for air. But now, it was up to me.

I blew my whistle, jumped in and swam to where the boy went under. Diving, I pulled him to the surface and used a cross-body rescue hold while talking calmly to him. Masking my own fears, I swam us toward the float. By that time Rod had rowed close and helped me get the boy into the boat. We wrapped him in a towel; his body shook with fright.

That evening I still felt a little numb from the experience, my first real rescue, and my mind kept replaying the event. I had done what needed doing in the moment because I knew how. I was a *real* lifeguard.

On my way to the dining hall, I ran into Benny.

Lifeguard

"I heard about your rescue this afternoon," he said. That showed a lot of courage. But then," he offered with a smile, "I always knew you were gutsy." Then he added, looking me straight in the eyes, "Hey, I'm sorry." •

Copyright 2024, Susan W. Harris

Susan W. Harris lives in Hilton Head, South Carolina, where she is a member of the Island Writers Network, (IWN). Her mother, a writer, encouraged her to write. Professionally she wrote grants and proposals for nonprofits. Poems and stories were published in the IWN anthology's recent two books. Currently, she is writing a novel inspired by the life of her grandmother and mother.

One by One: Defying the "Nevers"
by Emily Rosen

Yesterday my friend Beth came for a quickie visit and as I walked out the door with her, she mounted her bike, with a smiling *"toodle-oo."*

Aha! said I to my ancient self, *Good reminder! My bike!* It's been sitting there with pancake tires for much too long. *Time to get moving on it again.*

But, oh, the lagging path between words and actions!

Other people do yoga, meditation, mindfulness exercises, acupuncture, massage therapy, spiritual and religious immersions, and nature explorations to achieve nirvana and a way of coping with life stresses. I too indulge in much of that but at one time my major daily "go to" activity for swaying into bliss *had been* solo bike riding.

I never aspired to be a "tournament" bike rider. I wasn't into excessive speed or distance. My three-to-five-mile forays had always fulfilled my need. No bike clubs or groupie occasions. Happiness was just me on my rolling wheels, an occasional change of scenery and the exuberance of my freedom of movement.

The words "had been" scratch into my psyche and, when I allow it, awaken my angst. I had given up bike riding *temporarily*, I vowed, because I had succumbed to a self-protective anxiety attacking my confidence and my questionable reflexes.

For days I would stare at my bike, each time I entered my garage, thinking "Soon, soon, I will try it again. Maybe just a short whirl down the driveway, or a stop at the adjacent community. I wonder if the roofers in the community will remember me." I had often paused to engage them in conversation when their lunchtime coincided with my bike-break. Maybe—even probably—their job is completed by now. And then, my unruly mind would explode into unwinding the mysteries of the passing of time.

Thoughts about the bike had begun to wither at about the same pace as the withering of time. But I had never given up the hope of returning to it someday. For me, the motion of the bike was just the right pace, the passing landscapes although often familiar, held all kinds of mysteries which stirred my imagination, and my self-conversation provided all the soothing soulfulness I craved. Riding my bike has been a metaphor for all that I have held to be symbolic of living life on my own terms.

For practical purposes, that word "temporary" means "living in a fantasy world." As an "ancient," such is often the box into which we land. We "temporarily" give up myriad activities accompanied by the weak hope of someday returning to them.

However, on this day, I pulled my bike out of the garage and onto the parking lot, along with my car. I reached on the shelf for the electric inflator which I then plugged into the lighter of my "running" vehicle and brought forth a low step stool to soften the effects of my arthritic back as I bent over to remove the screw-top into which the inflater cable pumped air. My fingers, despite their long-lost dexterity, eventually managed to unscrew each top successively, after some time. What would have required five minutes of ordinary adult time was accomplished in totality, in about two hours. I returned all parts to their rightful places as my bike remained, with fully inflated tires, daring me to mount it.

But by then, the sun had quietly sneaked into the depths of the horizon, Eastern Standard time, not yet a day old. Certainly, I was not about to venture into the dark night on a vehicle that was—well, let's face it—unsteady. No harm to wait for another "Florida Sunshine" day.

Or another.

Or another.

So far, several days have passed. Honest, I have been legitimately busy. I am not at all ignoring my bike. Each time, just before sliding into my yellow car, I stop by my bike and talk into its ear, watching its deep orange colors vibrate in anticipation, as I spew happy assurances that the day will soon arrive. Surely, I know—how very well I know—that it is "now or never."

And you can tell by the tone in my voice that I am reluctant to add to the mounting *nevers*.

Tomorrow is the day! •

Copyright 2024, Emily Rosen

Emily Rosen, 97, lives in Boca Raton, Florida, where for over 20 years and until her 95th birthday, she instructed classes in memoir writing, publishing two anthologies of stories from her classes, and the book, *Who Am I?* For two decades until the local weekly newspaper folded in 2021, she wrote her column, "Everything's Coming Up Rosen." Her travel and feature articles have appeared nationwide. She has worked as a copy writer, travel writer, columnist, elementary and community college teacher, mental health counselor, and owner of the now defunct "singing telegram" company, Witty Ditty. Until January 2024, her poetry languished in the pages of a fat notebook, but some of it was recently released in *Lingering Over a Long Life: Selected Poems from My Journey (*available on Amazon.com.) Visit her at EmilyRosen424.com.

The Storm Upstream
by Bill Donohue

My name is Bill and I have Cancer! This could be the intro to my newly acquired five-step support group, but it's not. I'm a quiet one in the back. Our group moves slowly about the cancer center, seeking our queue for radiation and chemo, consultation, and pastoral care; no secret handshakes, no by-laws directing mission, vision, and strategic planning. Masks are a give-away, but they could represent family guarding us against infection or worse. You might not recognize us on the street. It's just another group occupying my mind and once again capturing that fleeting zeal for change.

Inside the cancer hallways are more private settings, where eyes give away an interest to engage histories and victories while other eyes are downcast, retreating, silent with worry and uncertainty. The chatty ones are hoping to ring that golden bell—*cured*. The silent ones know better and ponder lost dreams and those fleeting passions.

Everyone has a self-interest group or collection of motivators. If you've acquired an addiction or been evicted, you have a group. Maybe not a monthly newsletter or local lobbyist but an association with opinions and experience, debts, and duties. No cures, reparations, or sobriety bells to ring. No justice in sight for your team.

My newest group, the cancer folks, have a keen interest in cures and treatments and costs and access. Given a chance, they will tell their stories, and some have made it to the research centers, the insurance companies, and the halls of Congress. I'm all for them. I think they represent positive, world-wide models for change and scientific advancement. I sure hope so. *Go for it!*

It brings me to the question of what can only one person do—I mean, really? I once was challenged by a disability advocate to share all I and my local advocacy groups had done—recently—to make a difference. I ticked off with pride legislative contacts, rally numbers, and press clippings. "How's it working for ya?" he asked with sarcasm. He knew my answer and saw my shoulders drop.

"Hey," he said, "the only real difference we make is when we chain our chairs to the pillars and storm the palace! We sit and shout, we expose, educate, and demand! Helen Keller on fire!"

People know about Cancer. There are lung, breast, and support groups galore, connected with Big Pharma, academia, and hospital associations. We don't need ice plunges or lapel buttons. People are working for us, even the President.

Still, unhoused people, climate immigrants, uninsured and vulnerable exist unrepresented across all racial and cultural backgrounds. When will it be too late to make their difference heard?

What of the four generations of radiation victims still unrecognized by lawmakers and filmmakers following the Trinity Project and *Oppenheimer* filming in New Mexico?

What of the Oak Flat Apache who see their sacred lands surrounded once again by unemployed miners, legislators and foreign manufacturers salivating for copper and other minerals under a treaty-protected homeland?

What of the 17,000 people with intellectual and developmental disabilities in North Carolina who face two decades of legislative intransigence as they wait for services, many in the prime years of life; many who will outlive desperate parent needs for their housing and direct care?

When I was called on years ago to chirp for the United Way on myriad worthy causes, their admonition was always to go "upstream" to solve problems. They liked my "crippled children's" stories. They made a vital, short-term difference to our local pocketbooks. But thinking upstream for them only meant early intervention or birth control.

Another admonition came from Maya Angelou: "Is this the hill you want to die on?" How far would you go to challenge or embarrass the powers that be and risk your access and influence? These kids will not always be cute and someday may want jobs and marriage and college … and curb cuts!

The Storm Upstream

Few people in any group can plant a flag, link a chain, or barnstorm a palace knowing it is their last and sweetest hill, wondering all the way, "Will I make a difference…*the* difference?" Is the time finally right?

Having a support group does not a political party make. Being 80 years old does not offer the fully fueled passion you'd like to undergird a storm upstream to the palace and take the hill—finally to make that difference in the lives of people with disabilities. But living with the unknowns of cancer might. •

Copyright 2024, Bill Donohue

Bill Donohue is a retired Dean of Students from Winston Salem, North Carolina, who shares a lifelong advocacy for people with disabilities. This story chronicles that passion with his own present-day battle with Cancer.

Out of Sight, Out of Mind
by Erika Hoffman

I assumed I'd spend my junior year at Duke University abroad. I'd studied French in high school and had done well. I scored high on the SAT achievement test in French. Much more gifted at reading and writing French than I was speaking or listening to it, I figured a year abroad was inevitable if I chose to major or minor in it. At college, I chose courses that were not difficult for me—literature courses. In retrospect, I'd have been smarter to sign up for subjects I found challenging, like chemistry.

My public high school in New Jersey placed me in Honors Chemistry. The whole class was guys except for one other gal. Our teacher told us repeatedly he had a doctorate from Yale; he thought it motivating to return our tests in *ascending* order. Diane and I competed to see who in the class would be the first to receive an exam back, the lowest grade. We felt gleeful if we placed third when Dr. Tilley returned the results. Ergo, in college I avoided Chemistry, like the plague! I took Rocks for Jocks. Not that I was interested in geology, but I could memorize the names and looks of stones, and I did like the scenery in that class.

My plan was to head to France my junior year. In January of my sophomore year, I had a blind date. My sorority sister was seeing a guy who didn't have a car, but his roommate had a Firebird. She was tasked with finding his roomie a blind date for the basketball game. Back then, we could just saunter into Cameron Stadium. There was no Coach K, Krzewski-ville, or Cameron Crazies. I don't recall much about that night except my blind date was from Georgia and didn't open the car door for me, which I found peculiar because one thing about Southern guys is they always opened doors for their dates. Even my high school boyfriends in New Jersey opened the door for me. This arranged date didn't talk much. I wondered if he'd been cajoled into going. At any rate, when we entered, I bumped into lots of PIKEs and KA frat boys I knew and waved to others across the court.

We sat on the bleachers like gargoyles except I was a grinning gargoyle because I'd exchanged greetings with so many folks. The teams began playing. I didn't pay attention. I scanned the stands to see who else I knew. At halftime, Duke was losing. My date made some derogatory statement: *Duke was certain to lose—again.* I became contrary. I blurted out: "Nope. The Blue Devils will win." I based this on nothing. I didn't even understand basketball, nor did I know how to gauge a team's skill. I exclaimed this assertion because I was taught to root for the home team—no matter what.

"Want to bet on that?" my date asked.

"Sure."

"A pitcher of beer?" he inquired.

"Deal."

I cheered on the team. Surprising us all, Duke pulled it out. Duke won, and I won a pitcher of beer.

I don't remember details now except that he picked me up the following Tuesday to treat me to beer at the Hofbrau Haus. I remembered then he was a Chemistry major and a junior and didn't belong to a fraternity.

When I returned that evening to my dormitory, some gals asked me who the cute guy was who picked me up that evening. Back then, your date had to sign in. The lobby was full of curious gawkers loitering about.

"Brian, I think. Or Byron? From Georgia. Yeah, Byron. *Lord Byron*, maybe."

I dated him the rest of that semester. Summer came. I knew I was going to France in the fall. But now, I wasn't so sure I wanted to leave. That July, he invited me down to Atlanta. I went. I met his family.

Maybe a semester abroad wasn't so long. *Should I go? Or stay?* He'll probably find another girlfriend while I'm in Aix-en-Provence, I figured. Then, I thought I'll probably never have this opportunity again. If I don't go, will I regret it forever? After college, there will be responsibilities, …. On and on the conundrum churned.

Out of Sight, Out of Mind

I left Labor Day. No phone calling long distance back then—too expensive. Letters only. Other girls with me on that sojourn lost track of their sweethearts. Thanksgiving passed. Christmas passed.

The end of January, I flew back to quaint Raleigh-Durham airport, which back then had the luggage carrousel outside. There, waiting for me, was my handsome blind date from Georgia.

Now or never? Turned out it was "forever." Four adult kids and nine grandchildren later, we live down the road from where we met, and sometimes drive to our alma mater to see a basketball game. He's never rooted against *our* team again! •

Copyright 2024, Erika Hoffman

Erika Hoffman is a happy and longtime resident of beautiful North Carolina. She's a member of three writing clans: North Carolina Writers Network; The Triangle Area Freelancers; and Carteret Writers. During the past 14 years while pursuing "her scrivener dream," she has succeeded in getting published 460 times. Yet, Erika deems her best achievement— besides being married forever—is having raised four functioning citizens. Without a doubt, her proudest moniker is "Ama" to six grandsons and three granddaughters.

Experiments in the Chemistry of Belonging
by Paula Teem Levi

I chose teaching as a second career through the encouragement from family, friends, and other teachers. After completing an Educator Preparation Course, I accepted a job teaching science to 9th-grade students. I was eager, but also a little nervous, about starting my first year of teaching.

During the first quarter, I discovered my science lesson plans were not connecting with my students. The results from several weekly tests disappointed me. I began to question my competence. My commitment to teaching wavered some. I shared my concerns with the principal.

The principal told me that new teachers often felt overwhelmed and challenged during the first year of teaching. And she shared that she and the other staff members still thought I was the best candidate to teach this class. She also had a challenge for me. A local corporation wanted to fund a new science lab for the school and to let the students design it. The principal wanted me to stay until Christmas break to get the science lab completed. After that, I could change to another class, if I wanted.

The principal then opened up a file with background stories on the young people in the class. I learned a lot about my students. One, David, had a high IQ. He was caring for his younger siblings while his mother worked two jobs. His father had left the family years ago and was now serving a prison term. This helped explain why David spent so much time sleeping through class.

Learning the other students' stories, I began to realize that several of them also had struggles to deal with at home. All these factors influenced not only how the students were able to learn but told me how I needed to instruct them.

The following Monday morning, I arranged a trip for the students to see another school that had a new science lab. The students were in awe of the science lab they visited. So, everyone was excited when I told them that our class had been chosen to design a science lab for our school.

After returning to class, I asked David to lead a group in designing the science lab. David sat up from his usual slumped posture and seemed to take on a new demeanor. He worked diligently with the group on a floor plan. The following week, he proudly presented the floor plan on behalf of the group for approval by the class. The students voted unanimously to accept the proposed design. Their excitement created more excitement.

We divided the students into planning groups. I monitored the progress of each group by watching and listening. I was only involved in putting decisions together at the end of the class period for the entire class to vote on. The forming of new friendships in the class made a difference in the class environment, too.

Teachers, parents, and maintenance staff contributed their time after school and on weekends painting, installing new lighting, and creating storage spaces for equipment and hazardous materials in the lab. But delays in the shipment of equipment meant the lab was not completed by the Christmas break. Again, I had to choose to stay or not until the completion of the project. I stayed.

We completed the science lab in the spring and scheduled an open house viewing three weeks before the end of the school year. Each student received a new white lab coat and name badge to wear. David greeted each teacher and student at the door to the lab. He handed each visitor a brochure with a copy of the floor plan for the lab. The other class members guided the guests through the different workstations of the lab. They demonstrated different experiments using the newly purchased equipment.

David's mother and siblings, other students' family members, and the president of the corporation which donated money for the project also attended. I stood on the sidelines and beamed with pride at this little class of fledgling scientists. Everyone felt that our lab created an environment that was inviting and would have a positive impact on the well-being of the students and staff.

At the end of the year, all the students met the National and State Standard Requirements for science for advancement to the 10th grade. Our class had focused on creating a community where every student felt a sense of belonging. I felt that I was a part of this community, as well. The little community helped me to realize that there were new experiences, discoveries, and achievements available in pursuing a teaching career. So, I stayed. I'm glad I did. •

Copyright 2024, Paula Teem Levi

Paula Teem Levi is a retired Registered Nurse living in Clover, South Carolina. She is a member of several genealogical societies. Her stories have appeared in several previous anthologies of the Personal Story Publishing Project. Two stories have been published in the *Journal of Burke County (N.C.) Genealogical Society*. Paula's goal is to preserve as many stories as possible for future generations so that they will not be at risk of being forgotten or lost forever.

Do I Dare?
by Suzanne Cottrell

Prismatic mirages drift on the steamy asphalt of Indiana State Road 227. My three younger siblings and I hang out the windows of the 1964 Ford station wagon, but the rushing air provides little relief from the August heat. We tire of singing "Zip-A-Dee-Doo-Dah" to keep our mom awake. She clutches the steering wheel with her right hand and rubs her eyes with her left after driving eight hours. Our grandparents' farm is about an hour away. As Mom backs her foot off the accelerator pedal, she steers to the grassy shoulder.

"Why are we stopping?" Monotonous fields of corn and soybeans surround us.

Our mom turns toward me. Dark circles encompass her bloodshot eyes. "You've got to drive. If you don't, I'll run into the ditch."

"Really? With my learner's permit?" I drum my feet on the floorboard with excitement. But my stomach gets queasy.

"This stretch of road runs straight for miles." Mom winks. As she braces against the car hood and walks to the passenger door, my legs stick when I slide across the bench seat.

Do I Dare?

My siblings, my navigational scouts, shout, "All clear!"

As I ease my right foot onto the gas pedal, the car creeps like a tortoise. I press harder; the car jerks. Mom lifts her head, pats the seat, "Easy does it," and drifts to sleep.

"Sorry." I lick my lips and swallow hard. My eyes dart.

My siblings bounce on the back seat. "Can't you go faster!"

"Shhh, you'll wake Mom." The speedometer reads 35 mph. My trembling hands cause too much play in the steering wheel, and the car zigzags.

My siblings wobble. "Whoa!"

Maybe this isn't a good idea after all, but Mom's depending on me. My fingers ache as I grasp tighter, steady the car, and glance at the increasing speedometer. "Oh, no! What's that?" My eyes focus through the bug splattered windshield.

A monstrous piece of farm equipment lurches from a cornfield. Stalks dangle from the T-Rex's metal teeth as it crawls along the road. The beast grumbles and obscures my vision. "We'll never get to Grandpa and Grandma's in time for supper." I'd only passed one car while taking driver's ed. My shoulder and arm muscles tighten. *I've got to get around it.* A multitude of checklist items floods my brain: scan for a clear line of vision, calculate the distance, check the mirrors, signal my intent to pass, accelerate. When I pull into the left lane, I squint and hold my breath.

"Watch out." My sister grips the front seat back.

My pulse races when I spot a pickup truck heading toward us.

My older of two younger brothers waves his arm. "Punch it." Gripping the steering wheel, my leg trembles. I stomp on the brake.

"Hey, I said punch it."

I shake my head. "I know, but." Tires squeal, and the smell of burnt rubber wafts through the car. My siblings jostle and complain. Mom jerks awake. "What's wrong?"

That was close. My voice quivers as I explain, but Mom directs me not to pass. "The combine will turn off in a few minutes." After she nods, she closes her eyes.

I huff. *I blew it. More speed, but no, I hit the brakes.* The farm equipment drags ahead. My fingers tap on the steering wheel while my gaze fixes on the turf-green monster. *Can't you go any faster?* Once my hands are still, and I'm sure my mom is asleep, in a soft voice, I ask my brother, who's hanging out the window, "Can you see anything coming?"

"Nope."

My younger brother whines, "Mom said no passing."

"Yeah, but don't you want to get to Grandma and Grandpa's?" I glimpse him nodding when I check the rearview mirror. *Got to get around it.* I engage the left turn signal and pull into the passing lane. Our car is an ant beside the monstrous machine. *Come on, move over.* Instead, the harvester extends across the middle line. *Watch out. He can't see us.* As I swerve left, I cringe

Do I Dare?

and bite my lip. "Ouch!" *More gas, more gas.* My body shudders and sweat drips into my eyes. *What if those claws scratch our car?* I rehear the scritches when I drove our VW Bug too close to the poplar branches by the driveway. *Thank goodness. He's moving over. Keep going.* The beast appears in the rearview mirror. 1, 2, 3, clear. I made it, so I whip into the right lane. *Maintain speed, control.*

Mom awakes bleary-eyed. "Pull over. I'll drive now."

My siblings smack the back of the front seat. "Yeah. Mom's turn."

I nod and take a deep breath. Then I ease our station wagon onto the shoulder and sigh. *Yep, more practice, but I passed the green monster.* I grin. *Thanks Mom.* •

Copyright 2024, Suzanne Cottrell

Suzanne Cottrell, a member of the Taste Life Twice Writers and NC Writers' Network, lives with her husband in Granville County, NC. An outdoor enthusiast and retired teacher, she enjoys reading, writing, knitting, hiking, and Pilates. Her prose has appeared in numerous journals and anthologies, including the Personal Story Publishing Project, Inwood Indiana Press, Quillkeepers Press, and *Parks and Points*. She's the author of three poetry chapbooks: *Gifts of the Seasons, Autumn and Winter*; *Gifts of the Seasons, Spring and Summer*; and *Scarred Resilience*; and *Nature Calls Outside My Window, A Collection of Poems and Stories*. www.suzanneswords.com

This story involves a suicide.

Oh, My Son
by David M. Stern

Just minutes ago, searching the house to find you.
    Not in your bed. Not in the living room.
    Nowhere on the first floor. Not in the backyard.

For years, behaviors we could not fathom, unexplained appearances and disappearances.
    Glimmers of insight with moments of darkness.
    Being at home without finding a home.
    Talking without communicating.

Your flashes of humor and color, spontaneity and creativity.
    A cream pie with fresh berries—one bite better than the next.
    A spirit suffusing joy into any ambiance.

A jigsaw puzzle whose pieces don't fit without a blueprint for the masterplan.
    A design beyond our ability to comprehend.
    Maybe in four or more dimensions
    Maybe boring down along the path of a great screw

Months to decode why the pain, where the pain, how to palliate the pain.

Oh, My Son

No discoverable cause. No idea how to cure.
No secret salve to assuage. No solace in sight.

But pain still abounds—waxing and waning, but never departing, haunting another soul.

Then an abrupt absence from school and return home as an exile.
> Separation from friends. Separation from colleagues invested in your success.
> Separation from the environment in which you thrived.

Back home to us in a city not your own; your two parent-doctors not up to the task.
> A house filled with well-meaning but disconnected love.
> A maze leading inward with no exit from an inexplicable pain.
> A solo flight on an uncharted path through a typhoon.

Another round of medical studies, at our behest. Unrelenting commitment, efforts to cure.

A concrete approach—just like all the others.
> Too little. Too late.
> Not to happen. Nothing to say.

You, our son who found no hope.
> Surrounded by love and care unable to penetrate the hurt.
> Sitting quietly, clandestinely typing notes.

NOW OR NEVER

Vaguely disguised epitaphs chanting—all will be fine
—days will continue to pass.

Walking down the basement stairs. Dread spinning in my head
and smashing against the confines of my skull.
    A sight not to be seen. A thought not to be conceived.
    A moment never to have occurred.
    A discovery seared into our minds crowding out
        everything else—forever more.

It is never too late.   Until it is.
It is never impossible. Until it is.
Everything is possible. Until it isn't.

The implements of your destruction by your side.
    In the basement. Comfortably positioned.
    Morning sunlight through the window
        framing the scene.

Lifeless. Hope cast aside in a garbage bin by the door.
    If only this were a dream. It can't be real.
    Not in our repertoire. The very definition
        of irreversibility.

Your choice between two paths was no path.
    No path is not a choice of hope. No turning back
        from no path.
    We never conceived of no path.

A family cleaved by a sharp fissure surrounding
a gaping chasm.

Oh, My Son

> A schism that cannot be bridged.
> Spectators in life unable to act before the curtain falls.
> Sentenced to wander in an enchanted garden, unable to grasp that around us.
> Lost

Nothing ever the same. A lens that diminishes everything in its view.
> An elixir depleted, graying the outside world.
> Smoldering as it burns inside and out.
> No what ifs. No what's next. That's what definitive is.

Ashes spread over the clear waters of a lake.
> Floating effortlessly. Freed from agony and
>> misunderstanding.
> Swimming deep and shallow, Following a path
>> that only you know.

Oh, my son, if only… •

Copyright 2024, David M. Stern

The lives of David M. Stern, a physician-scientist and healthcare executive, and his wife, Kathleen Stern, an ophthalmologist, were jolted into a new reality by their younger son, Alan, who struggled with mental health and substance abuse problems. Alan's suicide, the subject of David's poem, was the single event that turned their lives upside down. David now cares for patients with mental health and substance use problems. His goal is to prevent other families from suffering the same loss as his own. David can be reached by email at dmstern85@gmail.com. •

What If?
by Landis Wade

A framed quote hangs on the wall in my writing space: "Courage to risk failure is what leads to success." My college football coach often repeated the phrase to our team, but I didn't need the motivation because I was committed to my teammates. It would have taken more courage to quit than to keep going. That was not the case in my mid-50s when I toyed with the idea of publishing a novella, a solo sport with which I had no prior experience. The idea of publishing a book was daunting, begging an answer to the question: *Would the courage to risk failure lead to writer success?*

Spoiler alert. Ten years later, I am not a New York Times bestselling author. I do not have a literary agent. My books are not traditionally published. And I struggle to make a profit. From a commercial standpoint, I have failed as a writer, but based on more than 500 interviews I've done with writers about their books, stories, and writing lives, I've learned that when it comes to being successful, "one size does not fit all."

Don't get me wrong. I would love to have my books consumed by millions of readers, worldwide, but that's a high bar. I recommend instead the advice of one writer who said:

What If?

"if your expectations are reasonable, lower them." I also recommend asking the question: *What if?*

What if I had never written my first book? It's like asking Jimmy Stewart what life would be like in Bedford Falls if he had never lived. If I had not written my first book, I would not have written the next one or the next one, nor would I have experienced the challenge and joy of putting books into the world. More importantly, I would not have met an engaging community of writers, like those who submit to the Personal Story Publishing Project. The PSPP editor told me, "I was in my 50s before I really discovered what it was I was supposed to be doing." In short, if I had not had the courage to risk failure as a writer in my 50s, my life would be less interesting and less friendly today. Like another writer told me, "If I knew it was so much fun being friends with writers, I wouldn't have bothered with people who aren't."

A writer I respect has those who attend her writing workshops to introduce themselves this way: *My name is Landis, and I am a writer.* In one sense, it's a confession. In another, it's an affirmation. In her mind, and in mine, if you write, you are a writer. An award-winning writer told me that "persistence beats patience every time." It's true. The status quo is easy. *Not* writing is easy. It takes courage to write, to accept feedback, to write to completion, and to put stories into the world to have them judged. Because if you get enough reviews, the one-star reviews will come, like the one I got when the reader didn't like my global warming plotline in one of my Christmas themed books, calling it "what Al Gore would like to read to his grandchildren on Christmas Eve; author Landis Wade has brought the *Inconvenient Truth* to the holiday season."

As I look back, I was fortunate to take two risks, not one. In addition to trying my hand at writing, I tried podcasting. I did not know the difference between a mixing bowl and a mixing board, but it didn't stop me from interviewing authors. Had I not done that, I would not have learned from bestselling author David Baldacci that "just because I've written all these books doesn't mean I'm ever going to master this craft of writing." Nor would I have learned from other bestselling authors that "a big part of this game is falling flat on your face;" "rejection happens to everyone;" and "the thing that is necessary for a writer if he's going to survive is to realize that the bottom doesn't last forever, and the top doesn't last forever."

The last ten years have taught me to believe in the quote on my wall. Courage to risk failure does lead to success, but only if we are open to the possibility of a different kind of success than we hoped for, like the result of that unanswered prayer in a country music song.

A few months before he passed away, North Carolina literary hall of fame writer Anthony Abbott said to me that "writing is not about writing, necessarily; writing is about living, and the more deeply and fully you live, the more you're able to write."

I am glad I sprung from the high dive of life into the deep end of writing.

The cannonball was a success. •

What If?

Copyright 2024, Landis Wade

Landis Wade writes light-hearted legal thrillers, mysteries, and essays. He is a recovering trial lawyer and host of Charlotte Readers Podcast where he has conducted more than 500 author interviews. His recent novel–*Deadly Declarations*–has won ten awards, including Winner in the 2022 American Fiction Awards and the National Indie Excellence Awards in the mystery categories. In 2023, he released *The Write Quotes* series–8 books on writing that feature inspirational and practical quotes from 500+ author interviews in 33 U.S states and five countries. His essays have appeared in six earlier anthologies by the Personal Story Publishing Project.

You Done Gone This Far
by Vicki Easterly

Nineteen years was a long time, just one year shy of full retirement benefits. The early years in state government had been good ones. We were young, fairly smart, and wildly funny. At least we thought we were.

It was at work that I took up with Tommy, an educated farm boy, who was witty and cute. The only problem was he had a roving eye. I pretended not to notice, because I did not want to notice. They were just dalliances anyway. We both loved Willie Nelson, riding in his blue Chevy pick-up truck, and trips to Nashville. We spent our lunch hours sitting by Daniel Boone's grave, which was across from our office in Frankfort, Kentucky. Our friends Ellie, Bryant, and Donna Faye sat with us. Those were the carefree days—before things changed.

Our job was to determine which of our claimants were eligible for Social Security disability benefits. I hated the denials. We recognized our decisions meant life or death to some.

Speaking of death, Donna Faye was diagnosed with malignant melanoma while we were still in our 30s. She only lasted a few painful months. The office went grievously quiet after she died.

Tommy and I lasted eight years. Shortly after Donna died, a new girl came to work. This time his roving eye was more than a dalliance. It was the end of us. Seeing them together every day was more than I could bear. I sank into a profound depression and took to my bed for a few months. Eventually I recovered.

I came back to work and stayed another 10 years, but it was never the same. Our group disbanded. I made new friends. We laughed and joked and even dressed up every Halloween. Though our usual dress code was jeans, one Halloween we dressed as power-hungry executives and had lunch at a swanky restaurant. We were so convincing with our briefcases and fake intellectual conversations that no one guessed we were in costume.

As the years went by, the work became more monotonous, the beige cubicles more confining, too many rules and regulations. I was bored; I was tired; my ADHD was making it more difficult to stay at my desk. Lunch hour became two hours. I knew it was wrong, but I could not stand being cooped up any longer.

An idea formed in my head and grew stronger as the weeks passed. I even had dreams about it at night. I wanted to quit my job and start my own business. Instead of denying claimants, I wanted to represent claimants and help them win their disability benefits. *But was that possible?* That had never been done in Frankfort. To qualify to be a non-attorney representative, I would be required to travel to Baltimore and to take a proficiency test, one based on my experience as a disability determiner. Only then could I represent clients before judges. Still, the urge became stronger as I became more miserable at work. After much praying, agonizing, and discussing it with my dad, I still did not know what to do.

One Saturday I visited Dad at his farm. Over coffee, I asked him one more time if he thought I should start my business, certain he would give me a final "no," and my dream would pass forever. Instead, he simply said, "Yep, you done gone this far." Although he sometimes used poor grammar, he was very intelligent and had become a successful entrepreneur himself, so he knew the challenges I would face. When he was sure, I was sure. Dad even co-signed on a start-up loan.

I found a pretty office downtown with trees outside my windows—windows, instead of beige walls. I painted my office a cozy terra cotta and hung pretty pictures. I waited for clients. Soon enough they began coming, many of them, in fact. I was not going to starve. *Whew.*

Next door to my office was Marshall's Restaurant, the diner where attorneys and business owners had lunch. Within two weeks, I had met there my future fiancé *new* Tom (not to be confused with *old* Tommy). Life was good again. I felt like a free bird, yet I worked harder and happier than ever. I had pride in my work, and I dressed in business suits. Once I was even mistaken for a judge! I made more money than I had ever imagined possible. Two years later, I married Tom, a man I would never have met if I had not made the decision to start my own business.

You Done Gone This Far

I could have stayed at my mundane job for another 10 years and lived a gray, soul-less, withering existence. I could have settled for "never," but thanks to my wise father, I chose "now," and to quote Robert Frost, "that has made all the difference." •

Copyright 2024, Vicki Easterly

Vicki Easterly lives in Frankfort, Kentucky. She is a retired disability advocate. Her short stories and memoirs have been published in various anthologies. She was a finalist in the 2021 Poetry Unites Kentucky essay contest. Her first book, *Miracles in The Mundane*, was selected for inclusion in the 2018 Kentucky Book Fair. She enjoys writing memoirs, essays, poetry and children's stories. She is a member of the Society of Children's Book Writers and Illustrators (SCBWI) and Bluegrass Writer's Coalition.

Philadelphia Duval— Taking the Plunge

by C. J. Munson

The facts about my ancestor's do-or-die decision are sparse, drawn from a few lines in a family history written in the 1930s, *DuVals of Kentucky from Virginia,* and some online sources. But one thing I know with reasonable certainty: over 300 years ago, Philadelphia Dubois DuVal made a drastic, life-altering choice to leave her home in France and everything she knew, and to move to America with her husband so they could live and worship in freedom.

Philadelphia Dubois was born in France around 1677 to a well-connected Catholic family. One of her uncles, the Abbé DuBois, was a powerful insider in the court of the King of France. It is all the more surprising, then, that she married Daniel DuVal, a Huguenot Protestant and a Chevalier to the King. Since the early 1500s, the Huguenot movement, inspired by the teachings of John Calvin, had spread quickly among the nobles, the intellectual elite, and skilled tradespeople. Fearful of losing political power, France's Catholic theocracy had alternated between tolerance and violent persecution of this religious minority. Perhaps Philadelphia followed her heart in marrying Daniel, or perhaps she, too, was persuaded by Calvin's teachings. But the Edict of Nantes, which had protected Protestants for nearly 100 years, had been revoked some years earlier, robbing them again of their religious freedom and civil rights. The tolerance that had made them more "French" than "Protestant" was replaced by a fear of the "Other" and a fanatical tribalism. Once again, their lives and freedom hung in the balance.

France was too dangerous for Daniel, who had already left for England. His bride, however, stayed behind for a time. Was she being watched? Would it have drawn too much attention for them to leave together? Or was she still weighing the cost of her decision? Did she believe, perhaps, that her family's connections would shield her from the worst?

The family history gives another tantalizing, even astonishing, detail about Philadelphia's departure: her own uncle, the Abbé Dubois, urged her to leave in disguise as a young male messenger of the King. He must have known she was in imminent danger. It was life or death, freedom or persecution. She chose freedom.

I imagine her waiting in the crowd near the harbor to board a ship for England. It must have felt odd to dress as a boy, to walk in trousers, to tuck her hair under a cap. But she did not leave empty-handed. The DuVal family history mentions some artifacts that she brought with her: a gold tureen and goblet set, likely a wedding gift, and a blue glass perfume bottle (The 1930s family history tells us that while the bottle was still in the family, the tureen and goblets had been sold through the "callous indifference of a much-disliked in-law.").

Whatever her feelings, whatever her hesitations, Philadelphia followed her conscience and sailed to London to join Daniel at the close of the 17th century. Then, in 1701, they left for Virginia on a ship named the *Nassau*. They joined a wave of half a million Protestants fleeing France for England, America, Holland, and Prussia. What France rejected, the world gained. In fact, so many American leaders were Huguenot descendants (e.g., George Washington, Paul Revere) that in 1787, patriot ally Marquis de Lafayette convinced Louis XVI to enact a law allowing religious freedom.

Philadelphia DuVal's single-minded decision to come to America bore much fruit. She and Daniel settled in Ware Parish, Gloucester County, Virginia. Welcomed by that community, they found safe harbor and put down roots. Like the majority of immigrants to America before and since, the DuVals were hard-working, responsible, grateful for the freedom and opportunity, and determined to make their family and their adoptive land proud.

Philadelphia bore five children. Several grandsons would become Revolutionary War officers. One DuVal connection, William Claiborne, an early Virginia colonial official, tangled with Lord Baltimore in a land dispute. A later descendant, Valentine Cook, is credited with creating the frontier revival meeting in the early 1800s. Others became farmers, governors, skilled craftspeople, doctors, teachers, and legislators, and, on the other side of the law, much later on, bootleggers and racketeers.

Philadelphia Duval—Taking the Plunge

Philadelphia did not live to see her children grow up, nor could she have imagined the wide-reaching impact her descendants would have. She passed away in 1715, at the age of 38, after bearing two children in the same year. But her tenacity in leaving France to come to America reverberates through the generations. For this brave woman, and for her courageous decision, her progeny are forever grateful. •

Copyright 2024, C. J. Munson

C. J. Munson lives part of the year in her hometown of Winston-Salem, NC. She is a wife, mother, sibling, and aunt who loves a good story. She hasn't written anything personal since high school, so this story was a pleasant change from work-related reports and articles. Post-retirement, she would love to investigate other tales passed down by the family *raconteurs*.

The Passing
by Randell Jones

The moment I had long feared was upon me in an instant. As I was closing my front door behind me, I discovered a firetruck and an ambulance of EMTs had just arrived next door at the home of my 100-year-old neighbor, Horace.

As I soon learned, his son-in-law had discovered Horace upstairs on the floor and called 911. He had visited Horace on Thursday; it was now Saturday. Horace could not talk coherently. He was dehydrated and weak from not eating for maybe two days. The EMTs cut off his clothes and loaded Horace into the ambulance. The son-in-law followed them. I stayed behind, promising I would lock up the house.

After a few days, I visited Horace in the ICU. He was still unconscious, hooked to all manner of monitors and tubes, unable to tell anyone what had happened. I stood there for awhile, taking in the moment, being present for him, I suppose.

Horace was a decorated veteran of World War II, having jumped before dawn on D-Day behind enemy lines with the 508th Regiment of the 82nd Airborne, fighting at Sainte-Mere-

Elglise. He later jumped into Nijmegen, Holland, and still later fought continually over two months through the Battle of the Bulge. Horace garnered four Purple Hearts and two Bronze Stars for his service and served as honor guard at Allied Headquarters in Frankfurt, Germany, greeting 5-star General Dwight Eisenhower every morning with a crisp salute, all before he was 22. But now Horace, at the century mark, had outlived all his friends and his bride of three-quarters of that journey so far. Surviving family members numbered few. Horace was attended mostly by hospital staff.

After learning that he was conscious but communicating with difficulty, I returned to visit Horace again. I brought along my copy of the book he wrote 20 years before about his war experiences. Standing beside his bed, I read the chapter I knew he would most enjoy, *if* he could hear me. It was a love story—their love story—how he met Gloria and courted her for just a month to begin their 74 years together. Horace was quiet while I read. I sat with him for an hour more, occasionally rubbing the bottoms of his feet, that human touch a gift for us both.

During another visit two days later, I touched Horace's right hand. He squeezed my thumb. I placed my right hand into the palm of his, avoiding the needles and tubes taped onto the back of it. He squeezed for a moment, his grip firm and manly—he offered me this handshake, which I returned. When I left the room, I offered as a punctuation to my departure, "Good-bye, Horace," my voice neither firm nor manly.

Some minutes after 6 p.m. that day, February 22, I received a call: "He's gone." The family invited me to walk with them as his remains were transported from the room. The son-in-law, his adult daughter, and I sat with Horace's body for a couple of hours, telling stories over his now still body, empty of pulse and vitality, relieved of the difficult struggle to breathe.

Close to midnight, we fell in behind the gurney which the nurses had draped with an American flag. They told us some of the staff wanted to pay their respects. The charge nurse pushed the gurney with Horace's remains along the hall at a slow and formal pace. The few nurses on duty in the ICU at that hour stood quietly at their stations as we processed by. Their regard was much appreciated. Theirs was a respectful gesture. But when the double doors ahead of us opened, we were stunned to see two dozen or more hospital staff members lining both sides of the long corridor ahead in silent, reverential tribute. Some had gathered to honor the WWII veteran they had met and cared for over these few short days. Some came because they had heard that a 100-year-old war hero had died. As the flag-draped gurney passed by, all that passed between the family and those bearing witness were the whispers of heartfelt *thank yous* from the family and the sincere expressions of deep gratitude offered to Horace by the solemn presence of each staff member.

These young people, in their 20's and 30's mostly, who threw themselves every day into grappling with life and death in providing medical care to strangers, were touching history, paying their respects to the last of the *Greatest Generation*, honoring someone the age of their great-grandparents, someone who had lived through a time and a struggle they had only read about, someone who had gone to war and risked his life and helped change the world *for them* without any assurance that he would survive his early 20s, let alone live a hundred years. They wanted to honor that courage when they had the opportunity to say *thank you*, and not miss the chance to say they had seen such a person as he passed from this life.

All that attention was much appreciated by the family, of course, but what I think Horace would have wanted those honoring him to know is that every generation is preparing this world for the next generation and that in their own time and in their own way they can be heroes too.

Godspeed, Horace, and thank you for your service. •

Copyright 2024, Randell Jones

Randell Jones is an award-winning writer about the pioneer and Revolutionary War eras and North Carolina history. During 25 years, he has written 150+ history-based guest columns for the Winston-Salem Journal. In 2017, he created the Personal Story Publishing Project and in 2019, the companion podcast, "6-minute Stories" to encourage other writers. He lives in Winston-Salem, North Carolina. Visit RandellJones.com and BecomingAmerica250.com.

www.ingramcontent.com/pod-product-compliance
Lightning Source LLC
Chambersburg PA
CBHW022103160426
43198CB00008B/331